DELUSI(AN INTERPRETATION IN THE LIGHT OF PSYCHOANALYSIS OF *GRADIVA*, A NOVEL, BY WILHELM JENSEN

BY
DR. SIGMUND FREUD

TRANSLATED BY
HELEN M. DOWNEY

PREFACE

To Dr. G. Stanley Hall, President of Clark University, who first called to my attention the charm of *Gradiva*, by Wilhelm Jensen, and suggested the possibility of the translation and publication combined with the translation of Freud's commentary, I am deeply grateful for his kindly interest and effort in connection with the publication of the book, and his assistance with the technical terms of psychopathology.

In this connection I am also indebted to Dr. Smith Ely Jelliffe, who gave many helpful suggestions as a result of his thorough reading of the manuscript of the commentary.

I wish also to express my profound appreciation to my friend, Miss M. Evelyn Fitzsimmons, for her generous help with the original manuscript and other valuable comments offered while she was reading the entire proof.

HELEN M. DOWNEY.

WORCESTER, MASS.

7

9

INTRODUCTION

Jensen's brilliant and unique story of *Gradiva* has not only literary merit of very high order, but may be said to open up a new field for romance. It is the story of a young archæologist who suffered a very characteristic mental disturbance and was gradually but effectively cured by a kind of native psychotherapeutic instinct, which probably inheres in all of us, but which in this case was found in the girl he formerly loved but had forgotten, and who restored at the same time his health and his old affection for her.

Perhaps the most extraordinary thing about the work is that the author knew nothing of psychotherapy as such, but wrought his way through the labyrinth of mechanisms that he in a sense rediscovered and set to work, so that it needed only the application of technical terms to make this romance at the same time a pretty good key to the whole domain of psychoanalysis. In a sense it is a dream-story, but no single dream ever began to be so true to the typical nature of dreams; it is a clinical picture, but I can think of no clinical picture that had its natural human interest so enhanced by a moving romance. *Gradiva* might be an introduction to psychoanalysis, and is better than anything else we can think of to popularize it.

It might be added that while this romance has been more thoroughly analysed than any other, and that by Freud himself, it is really only one of many which in the literature of the subject have been used to show forth the mysterious ways of the unconscious. It indicates that psychoanalysis has a future in literary criticism, if not that all art and artists have, from the beginning, more or less anticipated as they now illustrate it.

The translator is thoroughly competent and has done her work with painstaking conscientiousness, and she has had the great advantage of having it revised, especially with reference to the translation of technical terms from the German, by no less an eminent expert in psychotherapy than Dr. Smith Ely Jelliffe.

G. STANLEY HALL.

11

PART I
GRADIVA
A POMPEIIAN FANCY
BY
WILHELM JENSEN

13

GRADIVA

On a visit to one of the great antique collections of Rome, Norbert Hanold had discovered a bas-relief which was exceptionally attractive to him, so he was much pleased, after his return to Germany, to be able to get a splendid plaster-cast of it. This had now been hanging for some years on one of the walls of his work-room, all the other walls of which were lined with bookcases. Here it had the advantage of a position with the right light exposure, on a wall visited, though but briefly, by the evening sun. About one-third life-size, the bas-relief represented a complete female figure in the act of walking; she was still young, but no longer in childhood and, on the other hand, apparently not a woman, but a Roman virgin about in her twentieth year. In no way did she remind one of the numerous extant bas-reliefs of a Venus, a Diana, or other Olympian goddess, and equally little of a Psyche or nymph. In her was embodied something humanly commonplace—not in a bad sense—to a degree a sense of present time, as if the artist, instead of making a pencil sketch of her on a sheet of paper, as is done in our day, had fixed her in a clay model quickly, from life, as she passed on the street, a tall, slight figure, whose soft, wavy hair a folded kerchief almost 14completely bound; her rather slender face was not at all dazzling; and the desire to produce such effect was obviously equally foreign to her; in the delicately formed features was expressed a nonchalant equanimity in regard to what was occurring about her; her eye, which gazed calmly ahead, bespoke absolutely unimpaired powers of vision and thoughts quietly withdrawn. So the young woman was fascinating, not at all because of plastic beauty of form, but because she possessed something rare in antique sculpture, a realistic, simple, maidenly grace which gave the impression of imparting life to the relief. This was effected chiefly by the movement represented in the picture. With her head bent forward a little, she held slightly raised in her left hand, so that her sandalled feet became visible, her garment which fell in exceedingly voluminous folds from her throat to her ankles. The left foot had advanced, and the right, about to follow, touched the ground only lightly with the tips of the toes, while the sole and heel were raised almost vertically. This movement produced a double impression of exceptional agility and of confident composure, and the flight-like poise, combined with a firm step, lent her the peculiar grace.

Where had she walked thus and whither was she going? Doctor Norbert Hanold, docent of archæology, really found in the relief nothing noteworthy for his science. It was not a plastic production of great art of the antique times, but was essentially a Roman *genre* production, and he could not explain what quality in it had aroused his attention; he knew only that he had been 15attracted by something and this effect of the first view had remained unchanged since then. In order to bestow a name upon the piece of sculpture, he had called it to himself Gradiva, "the girl splendid in walking." That was an epithet applied by the ancient poets solely to Mars Gradivus, the war-god going out to battle, yet to Norbert it seemed the most appropriate designation for the bearing and movement of the young girl, or, according to the expression of our day, of the young lady, for obviously she did not belong to a lower class but was the daughter of a nobleman, or at any rate was of honourable family. Perhaps—her appearance brought the idea to his mind involuntarily—she might be of the family of a patrician ædile whose office was connected with the worship of Ceres, and she was on her way to the temple of the goddess on some errand.

Yet it was contrary to the young archæologist's feeling to put her in the frame of great, noisy, cosmopolitan Rome. To his mind, her calm, quiet manner did not belong in this complex machine where no one heeded another, but she belonged rather in a smaller place where every one knew her, and, stopping to glance after her, said to a companion, "That is Gradiva"—her real name Norbert could not supply—"the daughter of ——, she walks more beautifully than any other girl in our city."

As if he had heard it thus with his own ears, the idea had become firmly rooted in his mind, where another supposition had developed almost into a conviction. On his Italian journey, he had spent several weeks in Pompeii studying the ruins; 16and in Germany, the idea had suddenly come to him one day that the girl depicted by the relief was walking there, somewhere, on the peculiar stepping-stones which have been excavated; these had made a dry crossing possible in rainy weather, but had afforded passage for chariot-wheels. Thus he saw her putting one foot across the interstice while the other was about to follow, and as he contemplated the girl, her immediate and more remote environment rose before his imagination like an actuality. It created for him, with the aid of his knowledge of antiquity, the vista of a long street, among the houses of which were many temples and porticoes. Different kinds of business and trades, stalls, work-shops, taverns came into view; bakers had their breads on display; earthenware jugs, set into marble counters, offered everything requisite for household and kitchen; at the street corner sat a woman offering vegetables and fruit for sale from baskets; from a half-dozen large walnuts she had removed half of the shell to show the meat, fresh and sound, as a temptation for purchasers. Wherever the eye turned, it fell upon lively colours, gaily painted wall surfaces, pillars with red and yellow capitals; everything reflected the glitter and glare of the dazzling noonday sun. Farther off on a high base rose a gleaming, white statue, above which, in the distance, half veiled by the tremulous vibrations of the hot air, loomed Mount Vesuvius, not yet in its present cone shape and brown aridity, but covered to its furrowed, rocky peak with glistening verdure. In the street only a few people moved about, seeking shade wherever possible, for the scorching heat of the summer noon hour paralysed the usually bustling activities. There Gradiva walked over the stepping-stones and scared away from them a shimmering, golden-green lizard.

Thus the picture stood vividly before Norbert Hanold's eyes, but from daily contemplation of her head, another new conjecture had gradually arisen. The cut of her features seemed to him, more and more, not Roman or Latin, but Greek, so that her Hellenic ancestry gradually became for him a certainty. The ancient settlement of all southern Italy by Greeks offered sufficient ground for that, and more ideas pleasantly associated with the settlers developed. Then the young "domina" had perhaps spoken Greek in her parental home, and had grown up fostered by Greek culture. Upon closer consideration he found this also confirmed by the expression of the face, for quite decidedly wisdom and a delicate spirituality lay hidden beneath her modesty.

These conjectures or discoveries could, however, establish no real archæological interest in the little relief, and Norbert was well aware that something else, which no doubt might be under the head of science, made him return to frequent contemplation of the likeness. For him it was a question of critical judgment as to whether the artist had reproduced Gradiva's manner of walking from life. About that he could not become absolutely certain, and his rich collection of copies of antique plastic works did not help him in this matter. The nearly vertical position of the right foot seemed exaggerated; in all experiments which he himself made, the movement left his rising foot always in a much less upright position; mathematically formulated, his stood, during the brief moment of lingering, at an angle of only forty-five degrees from the ground, and this seemed to him natural for the mechanics of walking, because it served the purpose best. Once he used the presence of a young anatomist friend as an opportunity for raising the question, but the latter was not able to deliver a definite decision, as he had made no observations in this connection. He confirmed the experience of his friend, as agreeing with his own, but could not say whether a woman's manner of walking was different from that of a man, and the question remained unanswered.

In spite of this, the discussion had not been without profit, for it suggested something that had not formerly occurred to him; namely, observation from life for the purpose of enlightenment on the matter. That forced him, to be sure, to a mode of action utterly foreign to him; women had formerly been for him only a conception in marble or bronze, and he had never given his feminine contemporaries the least consideration; but his desire for knowledge transported him into a scientific passion in which he surrendered himself to the peculiar investigation which he recognized as necessary. This was hindered by many difficulties in the human throng of the large city, and results of the research were to be hoped for only in the less frequented streets. Yet, even there, long skirts generally made the mode of walking undiscernible, for almost no one but housemaids wore short skirts and they, with the exception of a few, because of their heavy shoes could not well be considered in solving the question. In spite of this he steadfastly continued his survey in dry, as well as in wet weather; he perceived that the latter promised the quickest results, for it caused the ladies to raise their skirts. To many ladies, his searching glances directed at their feet must have inevitably been quite noticeable; sometimes a displeased expression of the lady observed showed that she considered his demeanour a mark of boldness or ill-breeding; sometimes, as he was a young man of very captivating appearance, the opposite, a bit of encouragement, was expressed by a pair of eyes. Yet one was as incomprehensible to him as the other. Gradually his perseverance resulted in the collection of a considerable number of observations, which brought to his attention many differences. Some walked slowly, some fast, some ponderously, some buoyantly. Many let their soles merely glide over the ground;

3

not many raised them more obliquely to a smarter position. Among all, however, not a single one presented to view Gradiva's manner of walking. That filled him with satisfaction that he had not been mistaken in his archæological judgment of the relief. On the other hand, however, his observations caused him annoyance, for he found the vertical position of the lingering foot beautiful, and regretted that it had been created by the imagination or arbitrary act of the sculptor and did not correspond to reality.

Soon after his pedestrian investigations had yielded him this knowledge, he had, one night, a dream which caused him great anguish of mind. In it he was in old Pompeii, and on the 20 twenty-fourth of August of the year 79, which witnessed the eruption of Vesuvius. The heavens held the doomed city wrapped in a black mantle of smoke; only here and there the flaring masses of flame from the crater made distinguishable, through a rift, something steeped in blood-red light; all the inhabitants, either individually or in confused crowd, stunned out of their senses by the unusual horror, sought safety in flight; the pebbles and the rain of ashes fell down on Norbert also, but, after the strange manner of dreams, they did not hurt him, and in the same way, he smelled the deadly sulphur fumes of the air without having his breathing impeded by them. As he stood thus at the edge of the Forum near the Jupiter temple, he suddenly saw Gradiva a short distance in front of him. Until then no thought of her presence there had moved him, but now suddenly it seemed natural to him, as she was, of course, a Pompeiian girl, that she was living in her native city and, without his having any suspicion of it, was his contemporary. He recognized her at first glance; the stone model of her was splendidly striking in every detail, even to her gait; involuntarily he designated this as "lente festinans." So with buoyant composure and the calm unmindfulness of her surroundings peculiar to her, she walked across the flagstones of the Forum to the Temple of Apollo. She seemed not to notice the impending fate of the city, but to be given up to her thoughts; on that account he also forgot the frightful occurrence, for at least a few moments, and because of a feeling that the living reality would quickly disappear from him again, he tried 21 to impress it accurately on his mind. Then, however, he became suddenly aware that if she did not quickly save herself, she must perish in the general destruction, and violent fear forced from him a cry of warning. She heard it, too, for her head turned toward him so that her face now appeared for a moment in full view, yet with an utterly uncomprehending expression; and, without paying any more attention to him, she continued in the same direction as before. At the same time, her face became paler as if it were changing to white marble; she stepped up to the portico of the Temple, and then, between the pillars, she sat down on a step and slowly laid her head upon it. Now the pebbles were falling in such masses that they condensed into a completely opaque curtain; hastening quickly after her, however, he found his way to the place where she had disappeared from his view, and there she lay, protected by the projecting roof, stretched out on the broad step, as if for sleep, but no longer breathing, apparently stifled by the sulphur fumes. From Vesuvius the red glow flared over her countenance, which, with closed eyes, was exactly like that of a beautiful statue. No fear nor distortion was apparent, but a strange equanimity, calmly submitting to the inevitable, was manifest in her features. Yet they quickly became more indistinct as the wind drove to the place the rain of ashes, which spread over them, first like a grey gauze veil, then extinguished the last glimpse of her face, and soon, like a Northern winter snowfall, buried the whole figure under a smooth cover. Outside, the pillars of the Temple of Apollo rose, now, however, only 22 half of them, for the grey fall of ashes heaped itself likewise against them.

When Norbert Hanold awoke, he still heard the confused cries of the Pompeiians who were seeking safety, and the dully resounding boom of the surf of the turbulent sea. Then he came to his senses; the sun cast a golden gleam of light across his bed; it was an April morning and outside sounded the various noises of the city, cries of venders, and the rumbling of vehicles. Yet the dream picture still stood most distinctly in every detail before his open eyes, and some time was necessary before he could get rid of a feeling that he had really been present at the destruction on the bay of Naples, that night nearly two thousand years ago. While he was dressing, he first became gradually free from it, yet he did not succeed, even by the use of critical thought, in breaking away from the idea that Gradiva had lived in Pompeii and had been buried there in 79. Rather, the former conjecture had now

4

become to him an established certainty, and now the second also was added. With woful feeling he now viewed in his living-room the old relief which had assumed new significance for him. It was, in a way, a tombstone by which the artist had preserved for posterity the likeness of the girl who had so early departed this life. Yet if one looked at her with enlightened understanding, the expression of her whole being left no doubt that, on that fateful night, she had actually lain down to die with just such calm as the dream had showed. An old proverb says that the darlings of the gods are taken from the earth in the full vigour of youth.

23Without having yet put on a collar, in morning array, with slippers on his feet, Norbert leaned on the open window and gazed out. The spring, which had finally arrived in the north also, was without, but announced itself in the great quarry of the city only by the blue sky and the soft air, yet a foreboding of it reached the senses, and awoke in remote, sunny places a desire for leaf-green, fragrance and bird song; a breath of it came as far as this place; the market women on the street had their baskets adorned with a few, bright wild flowers, and at an open window, a canary in a cage warbled his song. Norbert felt sorry for the poor fellow for, beneath the clear tone, in spite of the joyful note, he heard the longing for freedom and the open.

Yet the thoughts of the young archæologist dallied but briefly there, for something else had crowded into them. Not until then had he become aware that in the dream he had not noticed exactly whether the living Gradiva had really walked as the piece of sculpture represented her, and as the women of to-day, at any rate, did not walk. That was remarkable because it was the basis of his scientific interest in the relief; on the other hand, it could be explained by his excitement over the danger to her life. He tried, in vain, however, to recall her gait.

Then suddenly something like a thrill passed through him; in the first moment he could not say whence. But then he realized; down in the street, with her back toward him, a female, from figure and dress undoubtedly a young lady, was walking along with easy, elastic step. Her dress, 24which reached only to her ankles, she held lifted a little in her left hand, and he saw that in walking the sole of her slender foot, as it followed, rose for a moment vertically on the tips of the toes. It appeared so, but the distance and the fact that he was looking down did not admit of certainty.

Quickly Norbert Hanold was in the street without yet knowing exactly how he had come there. He had, like a boy sliding down a railing, flown like lightning down the steps, and was running down among the carriages, carts and people. The latter directed looks of wonder at him, and from several lips came laughing, half mocking exclamations. He was unaware that these referred to him; his glance was seeking the young lady and he thought that he distinguished her dress a few dozen steps ahead of him, but only the upper part; of the lower half, and of her feet, he could perceive nothing, for they were concealed by the crowd thronging on the sidewalk.

Now an old, comfortable, vegetable woman stretched her hand toward his sleeve, stopped him and said, half grinning, "Say, my dear, you probably drank a little too much last night, and are you looking for your bed here in the street? You would do better to go home and look at yourself in the mirror."

A burst of laughter from those near by proved it true that he had shown himself in garb not suited to public appearance, and brought him now to realization that he had heedlessly run from his room. That surprised him because he insisted upon conventionality of attire and, forsaking his project, 25he quickly returned home, apparently, however, with his mind still somewhat confused by the dream and dazed by illusion, for he had perceived that, at the laughter and exclamation, the young lady had turned her head a moment, and he thought he had seen not the face of a stranger, but that of Gradiva looking down upon him.

Because of considerable property, Doctor Norbert Hanold was in the pleasant position of being unhampered master of his own acts and wishes and, upon the appearance of any inclination, of not depending for expert counsel about it on any higher court than his own decision. In this way he differed most favourably from the canary, who could only warble out, without success, his inborn impulse to get out of the cage into the sunny open.

Otherwise, however, the young archæologist resembled the latter in many respects. He had not come into the world and grown up in natural freedom, but already at birth had been hedged in by the grating with which family tradition, by education and predestination, had surrounded him. From his early childhood no doubt had existed in his parents' house that he, as the only son of a university professor and antiquarian, was called upon to preserve, if possible to exalt, by that very activity the glory of his father's name; so this business continuity had always seemed to him the natural task of his future. He had clung loyally to it even after the early deaths of his parents had left him absolutely alone; in connection with his brilliantly passed examination in [26]philology, he had taken the prescribed student trip to Italy and had seen in the original a number of old works of art whose imitations, only, had formerly been accessible to him. Nothing more instructive for him than the collections of Florence, Rome, Naples could be offered anywhere; he could furnish evidence that the period of his stay there had been used excellently for the enrichment of his knowledge, and he had returned home fully satisfied to devote himself with the new acquisitions to his science. That besides these objects from the distant past, the present still existed round about him, he felt only in the most shadowy way; for his feelings marble and bronze were not dead, but rather the only really vital thing which expressed the purpose and value of human life; and so he sat in the midst of his walls, books and pictures, with no need of any other intercourse, but whenever possible avoiding the latter as an empty squandering of time and only very reluctantly submitting occasionally to an inevitable party, attendance at which was required by the connections handed down from his parents. Yet it was known that at such gatherings he was present without eyes or ears for his surroundings, and as soon as it was any way permissible, he always took his leave, under some pretext, at the end of the lunch or dinner, and on the street he greeted none of those whom he had sat with at the table. That served, especially with young ladies, to put him in a rather unfavourable light; for upon meeting even a girl with whom he had, by way of exception, spoken a few words, he looked at her without a greeting as at a quite [27]unknown person whom he had never seen. Although perhaps archæology, in itself, might be a rather curious science and although its alloy had effected a remarkable amalgamation with Norbert Hanold's nature, it could not exercise much attraction for others and afforded even him little enjoyment in life according to the usual views of youth. Yet with a perhaps kindly intent Nature had added to his blood, without his knowing of the possession, a kind of corrective of a thoroughly unscientific sort, an unusually lively imagination which was present not only in dreams, but often in his waking hours, and essentially made his mind not preponderantly adapted to strict research method devoid of interest. From this endowment, however, originated another similarity between him and the canary. The latter was born in captivity, had never known anything else than the cage which confined him in narrow quarters, but he had an inner feeling that something was lacking to him, and sounded from his throat his desire for the unknown. Thus Norbert Hanold understood it, pitied him for it, returned to his room, leaned again from the window and was thereupon moved by a feeling that he, too, lacked a nameless something. Meditation on it, therefore, could be of no use. The indefinite stir of emotion came from the mild, spring air, the sunbeams and the broad expanse with its fragrant breath, and formed a comparison for him; he was likewise sitting in a cage behind a grating. Yet this idea was immediately followed by the palliating one that his position was more advantageous than that of the canary, for he had in his possession wings which [28]were hindered by nothing from flying out into the open at his pleasure.

But that was an idea which developed more upon reflection. Norbert gave himself up for a time to this occupation, yet it was not long before the project of a spring journey assumed definite shape. This he carried out that very day, packed a light valise, and before he went south by the night express, cast at nightfall another regretful departing glance on Gradiva, who, steeped in the last rays of the sun, seemed to step out with more buoyancy than ever over the invisible stepping-stones beneath her feet. Even if the impulse for travel had originated in a nameless feeling, further reflection had, however, granted, as a matter of course, that it must serve a scientific purpose. It had occurred to him that he had neglected to inform himself with accuracy about some important archæological questions in connection with some statues in Rome and, without stopping on the way, he made the journey of a day and a half thither.

Not very many personally experience the beauty of going from Germany to Italy in the spring when one is young, wealthy and independent, for even those endowed with the three latter requirements are not always accessible to such a feeling for beauty, especially if they (and alas they form the majority) are in couples on the days or weeks after a wedding, for such allow nothing to pass without an extraordinary delight, which is expressed in numerous superlatives; and finally they bring 29 back home, as profit, only what they would have discovered, felt or enjoyed exactly as much by staying there. In the spring such dualists usually swarm over the Alpine passes in exactly opposite direction to the birds of passage. During the whole journey they billed and cooed around Norbert as if they were in a rolling dove-cot, and for the first time in his life he was compelled to observe his fellow beings more closely with eye and ear. Although, from their speech, they were all German country people, his racial identity with them awoke in him no feeling of pride, but rather the opposite one, that he had done reasonably well to bother as little as possible with the *homo sapiens* of Linnæan classification, especially in connection with the feminine half of this species; for the first time he saw also, in his immediate vicinity, people brought together by the mating impulse without his being able to understand what had been the mutual cause. It remained incomprehensible to him why the women had chosen these men, and still more perplexing why the choice of the men had fallen upon these women. Every time he raised his eyes, his glance had to fall on the face of some one of them and it found none which charmed the eye by outer attraction or possessed indication of intellect or good nature. To be sure, he lacked a standard for measuring, for of course one could not compare the women of to-day with the sublime beauty of the old works of art, yet he had a dark suspicion that he was not to blame for this unkind view, but that in all expressions there was something lacking which ordinary life was in duty bound to offer. So he reflected for 30 many hours on the strange impulses of human beings, and came to the conclusion that of all their follies, marriage, at any rate, took the prize as the greatest and most incomprehensible one, and the senseless wedding trips to Italy somehow capped the climax of this buffoonery.

Again, however, he was reminded of the canary that he had left behind in captivity, for he also sat here in a cage, cooped in by the faces of young bridal couples which were as rapturous as vapid, past which his glance could only occasionally stray through the window. Therefore it can be easily explained that the things passing outside before his eyes made other impressions on him than when he had seen them some years before. The olive foliage had more of a silver sheen; the solitary, towering cypresses and pines here and there were delineated with more beautiful and more distinctive outlines; the places situated on the mountain heights seemed to him more charming, as if each one, in a manner, were an individual with different expression; and Trasimene Lake seemed to him of a soft blue such as he had never noticed in any surface of water. He had a feeling that a Nature unknown to him was surrounding the railway tracks, as if he must have passed through these places before in continual twilight, or during a grey rainfall, and was now seeing them for the first time in their golden abundance of colour. A few times he surprised himself in a desire, formerly unknown to him, to alight and seek afoot the way to this or that place because it looked to him as if it might be concealing something peculiar or mysterious. Yet he did not allow 31 himself to be misled by such unreasonable impulses, but the "diretissimo" took him directly to Rome where, already, before the entrance into the station, the ancient world with the ruins of the temple of Minerva Medica received him. When he had finally freed himself from his cage filled with "inseparables," he immediately secured accommodations in a hotel well known to him, in order to look about from there, without excessive haste, for a private house satisfactory to him.

Such a one he had not yet found in the course of the next day, but returned to his "albergo" again in the evening and went to sleep rather exhausted by the unaccustomed Italian air, the strong sun, much wandering about and the noise of the streets. Soon consciousness began to fade, but just as he was about to fall asleep he was again awakened, for his room was connected with the adjoining one by a door concealed only by a wardrobe, and into this came two guests, who had taken possession of it that morning. From the voices which sounded through the thin partition, they were a man and a woman who unmistakably belonged to that class of German spring birds of passage with whom he had yesterday journeyed hither from Florence. Their frame of mind seemed to give decidedly favourable testimony concerning the hotel cuisine, and it might be due to the good quality of a Castellin-romani wine that they exchanged ideas and feelings most distinctly and audibly in North German tongue:

"My only Augustus."

"My sweet Gretchen."

"Now again we have each other."

32"Yes, at last we are alone again."

"Must we do more sight-seeing to-morrow?"

"At breakfast we shall look in *Baedeker* for what is still to be done."

"My only Augustus, to me you are much more pleasing than Apollo Belvedere."

"And I have often thought, my sweet Gretchen, that you are much more beautiful than the Capitoline Venus."

"Is the volcano that we want to climb near here?"

"No, I think we'll have to ride a few hours more in the train to get there."

"If it should begin to belch flame just as we got to the middle, what would you do?"

"Then my only thought would be to save you, and I would take you in my arms—so."

"Don't scratch yourself on that pin!"

"I can think of nothing more beautiful than to shed my blood for you."

"My only Augustus."

"My sweet Gretchen."

With that the conversation ceased, Norbert heard another ill-defined rustling and moving of chairs, then it became quiet and he fell back into a doze which transported him to Pompeii just as Vesuvius again began its eruption. A vivid throng of fleeing people caught him, and among them he saw Apollo Belvedere lift up the Capitoline Venus, take her away and place her safely upon some object in a dark shadow; it seemed to be a carriage or cart on which she was to be carried off, for a rattling sound was soon heard from that direction. This mythological occurrence did not 33amaze the young archæologist, but it struck him as remarkable that the two talked German, not Greek, to each other for, as they half regained their senses, he heard them say:

"My sweet Gretchen."

"My only Augustus."

But after that the dream picture changed completely. Absolute silence took the place of the confused sound, and instead of smoke and fire-glow, bright, hot sunlight rested on the ruins of the buried city. This likewise changed gradually, became a bed on whose white linen golden beams circled up to his eyes, and Norbert Hanold awoke in the scintillating spring morning of Rome.

Within him, also, however, something had changed; why, he could not surmise, but a strangely oppressive feeling had again taken possession of him, a feeling that he was imprisoned in a cage which this time was called Rome. As he opened the window, there screamed up from the street dozens of venders' cries far more shrill to his ear than those in his German home; he had come only from one noisy quarry to another, and a strangely uncanny horror of antique collections, of meeting there Apollo Belvedere or the Capitoline Venus, frightened him away. Thus, after brief consideration, he refrained from his intention of looking for a dwelling, hastily packed his valise again and went farther south by train. To escape the "inseparables," he did this in a third-class coach, expecting at the same time to find there an interesting and scientifically useful company of Italian folk-types, the former models of antique works of art. Yet he found nothing but the usual 34dirt, Monopol cigars which smelled horribly, little warped fellows beating about with arms and legs, and members of the female sex, in contrast to whom his coupled country-women seemed to his memory almost like Olympian goddesses.

8

Two days later Norbert Hanold occupied a rather questionable space called a "room" in "Hotel Diomed" beside the eucalyptus-guarded "ingresso" to the excavations of Pompeii. He had intended to stay in Naples for some time to study again more closely the sculptures and wall-paintings in the Museo Nazionale, but he had had an experience there similar to that in Rome. In the room for the collection of Pompeiian household furniture he found himself wrapped in a cloud of feminine, ultra-fashionable travel-costumes, which had doubtless all quickly replaced the virgin radiance of satin, silk or lace bridal finery; each one clung to the arm of a young or old companion, likewise faultlessly attired, according to men's fashion standards; and Norbert's newly gained insight into a field of knowledge formerly unknown to him had advanced so far as to permit him to recognize them at first glance; every man was Augustus, every girl was Gretchen. Only this came to light here by means of other forms of conversation tempered, moderated and modified by the ear of publicity.

"Oh, look, that was practical of them; we'll surely have to get a meat warmer like that, too."

"Yes, but for the food that my wife cooks it must be made of silver."

35"How do you know that what I cook will taste so good to you?"

The question was accompanied by a roguish, arch glance and was answered in the affirmative, with a glance varnished with lacquer, "What you serve to me can be nothing but delicious."

"No; that surely is a thimble! Did the people of those days have needles?"

"It almost seems so, but you could not have done anything with that, my darling, it would be much too large even for your thumb."

"Do you really think that? And do you like slender fingers better than broad ones?"

"Yours I do not need to see; by touch I could discover them, in the deepest darkness, among all the others in the world."

"That is really awfully interesting. Do we still really have to go to Pompeii also?"

"No, that will hardly pay; there are only old stones and rubbish there; whatever was of value, *Baedeker* says, was brought here. I fear the sun there would be too hot for your delicate complexion, and I could never forgive myself that."

"What if you should suddenly have a negress for a wife?"

"No, my imagination fortunately does not reach that far, but a freckle on your little nose would make me unhappy. I think, if it is agreeable to you, we'll go to Capri to-morrow, my dear. There everything is said to be very comfortable, and in the wonderful light of the Blue Grotto I shall first realize completely what a great prize I have drawn in the lottery of happiness."

"You—if any one hears that, I shall be almost 36ashamed. But wherever you take me, it is agreeable to me, and makes no difference, for I have you with me."

Augustus and Gretchen over again, somewhat toned down and tempered for eye and ear. It seemed to Norbert Hanold that he had had thin honey poured upon him from all sides and that he had to dispose of it swallow by swallow. A sick feeling came over him, and he ran out of the Museo Nazionale to the nearest "osteria" to drink a glass of vermuth. Again and again the thought intruded itself upon his mind: Why did these hundredfold dualities fill the museums of Florence, Rome, Naples, instead of devoting themselves to their plural occupations in their native Germany? Yet from a number of chats and tender talks, it seemed to him that the majority of these bird couples did not intend to nest in the rubbish of Pompeii, but considered a side trip to Capri much more profitable, and thence originated his sudden impulse to do what they did not do. There was at any rate offered to him a chance to be freed from the main flock of this migration and to find what he was vainly seeking here in Italy. That was also a duality, not a wedding duality, but two members of the same family without cooing bills, silence and science, two calm sisters with whom only one could count upon satisfactory shelter. His desire for them contained something formerly unknown to him; if it had not been a contradiction in itself, he could have applied to this impulse the epithet "passionate"—and an hour later he was already sitting in a "carrozzella" which bore him through 37the interminable Portici and Resina. The journey was like one through a street splendidly adorned for an old Roman victor; to the right and left almost every house spread out to dry in the sun, like yellow tapestry hangings, a super-abundant wealth of "pasta di Napoli," the greatest dainty of the country, thick or thin macaroni, vermicelli, spaghetti, canelloni and fidelini, to which smoke of fats from cook-shops, dust-clouds, flies and fleas, the fish scales flying about in the air, chimney smoke and other day and night influences lent the familiar delicacy of its taste. Then the cone of Vesuvius looked down close by across brown lava fields; at the right extended the gulf of shimmering blue, as if composed of liquid malachite and lapis lazuli. The little nutshell on wheels flew, as if whirled forth by a mad storm and as if every moment must be its last, over the dreadful pavement of Torre del Greco, rattled through Torre dell'Annunziata, reached the Dioscuri, "Hotel Suisse" and "Hotel Diomed," which measured their power of attraction in a ceaseless, silent, but ferocious struggle, and stopped before the latter whose classic name, again, as on his first visit, had determined the choice of the young archæologist. With apparently, at least, the greatest composure, however, the modern Swiss competitor viewed this event before its very door. It was calm because no different water from what it used was boiled in the pots of its classic neighbour; and the antique splendours temptingly displayed for sale over there had not come to light again after two thousand years under the ashes, any more than the ones which it had.

38Thus Norbert Hanold, contrary to all expectations and intentions, had been transported in a few days from northern Germany to Pompeii, found the "Diomed" not too much filled with human guests, but on the other hand populously inhabited by the *musca domestica communis*, the common house-fly. He had never been subject to violent emotions; yet a hatred of these two-winged creatures burned within him; he considered them the basest evil invention of Nature, on their account much preferred the winter to the summer as the only time suited to human life, and recognized in them invincible proof against the existence of a rational world-system. Now they received him here several months earlier than he would have fallen to their infamy in Germany, rushed immediately about him in dozens, as upon a patiently awaited victim, whizzed before his eyes, buzzed in his ears, tangled themselves in his hair, tickled his nose, forehead and hands. Therein many reminded him of honeymoon couples, probably were also saying to each other in their language, "My only Augustus" and "My sweet Gretchen"; in the mind of the tormented man rose a longing for a "scacciamosche," a splendidly made fly-flapper like one unearthed from a burial vault, which he had seen in the Etruscan museum in Bologna. Thus, in antiquity, this worthless creature had likewise been the scourge of humanity, more vicious and more inevitable than scorpions, venomous snakes, tigers and sharks, which were bent upon only physical injury, rending or devouring the ones attacked; against the former one could guard himself by thoughtful 39conduct. From the common house-fly, however, there was no protection, and it paralysed, disturbed and finally shattered the psychic life of human beings, their capacity for thinking and working, every lofty flight of imagination and every beautiful feeling. Hunger or thirst for blood did not impel them, but solely the diabolical desire to torture; it was the "Ding an sich" in which absolute evil had found its incarnation. The Etruscan "scacciamosche," a wooden handle with a bunch of fine leather strips fastened to it, proved the following: they had destroyed the most exalted poetic thoughts in the mind of Æschylus; they had caused the chisel of Phidias to make an irremediable slip, had run over the brow of Zeus, the breast of Aphrodite, and from head to foot of all Olympian gods and goddesses; and Norbert felt in his soul that the service of a human being was to be estimated, above all, according to the number of flies which he had killed, pierced, burned up or exterminated in hecatombs during his life, as avenger of his whole race from remotest antiquity.

For the achievement of such fame, he lacked here the necessary weapon, and like the greatest battle hero of antiquity, who had, however, been alone and unable to do otherwise, he left the field, or rather his room, in view of the hundredfold overwhelming number of the common foe. Outside it dawned upon him that he had thereby done in a small way what he would have to repeat on a larger scale on the morrow. Pompeii, too, apparently offered no peacefully gratifying abode for his needs. To this idea was added, at least 40dimly, another, that his dissatisfaction was certainly caused not by his surroundings alone, but to a degree found its origin in him. To be sure, flies had always been very repulsive to him, but they had never before transported him into such raging fury as this. On account of the journey his nerves were undeniably in an excited and irritable condition, for which indoor air and overwork at home during the winter had probably begun to pave the way. He felt that he was out of sorts because he lacked something without being able to explain what, and this ill-humour he took everywhere with him; of course flies and bridal couples swarming *en masse* were not calculated to make life agreeable anywhere. Yet if he did not wish to wrap himself in a thick cloud of self-righteousness, it could not remain concealed from him that he was travelling around Italy just as aimless, senseless, blind and deaf as they, only with considerably less capacity for enjoyment. For his travelling companion, science, had, most decidedly, much of an old Trappist about her, did not open her mouth when she was not spoken to, and it seemed to him that he was almost forgetting in what language he had communed with her.

It was now too late in the day to go into Pompeii through the "ingresso." Norbert remembered a circuit he had once made on the old city-wall, and attempted to mount the latter by means of all sorts of bushes and wild growth. Thus he wandered along for some distance a little above the city of graves, which lay on his right, motionless and quiet. It looked like a dead rubbish field already almost covered with shadow, for the 41evening sun stood in the west not far from the edge of the Tyrrhenian Sea. Round about, on the other hand, it still bathed all the hilltops and fields with an enchanting brilliancy of life, gilded the smoke-cone rising above the Vesuvius crater and clad the peaks and pinnacles of Monte Sant' Angelo in purple. High and solitary rose Monte Epomeo from the sparkling, blue sea glittering with golden light, from which Cape Misenum reared itself with dark outline, like a mysterious, titanic structure. Wherever the gaze rested, a wonderful picture was spread combining charm and sublimity, remote past and joyous present. Norbert Hanold had expected to find here what he longed for vaguely. Yet he was not in the mood for it, although no bridal couples and flies molested him on the deserted wall; even nature was unable to offer him what he lacked in his surroundings and within himself. With a calmness bordering closely on indifference, he let his eyes pass over the all-pervading beauty, and did not regret in the least that it was growing pale and fading away in the sunset, but returned to the "Diomed," as he had come, dissatisfied.

But as he had now, although with ill-success, been conveyed to this place through his indiscretion, he reached the decision overnight, to get from the folly he had committed at least one day of scientific profit, and went to Pompeii on the regular road as soon as the "ingresso" was opened in the morning. In little groups commanded by official guides, armed with red *Baedekers* or their 42foreign cousins, longing for secret excavations of their own, there wandered before and behind him the population of the two hotels. The still fresh, morning air was filled almost exclusively by English or Anglo-American chatter; the German couples were making each other mutually happy with German sweets and inspiration up there on Capri behind Monte Sant' Angelo at the breakfast table of the Pagano. Norbert remembered how to free himself soon, by well chosen words, combined with a good "mancia," from the burden of a "guida," and was able to pursue his purposes alone and unhindered. It afforded him some satisfaction to know that he possessed a faultless memory; wherever his glance rested, everything lay and stood exactly as he remembered it, as if only yesterday he had imprinted it in his mind by means of expert observation. This continually repeated experience brought, however, the added feeling that his presence there seemed really very unnecessary, and a decided indifference took possession of his eyes and his intellect more and more, as during the evening on the wall. Although, when he looked up, the pine-shaped smoke-cone of Vesuvius generally stood before him against the blue sky, yet, remarkably, it did not once appear in his memory that he had dreamed some time ago that he had been present at the destruction of Pompeii by the volcanic eruption of 79. Wandering around for hours made him tired and half-sleepy, of course, yet he felt not the least suggestion of anything dreamlike, but there lay about him only a confusion of fragments of ancient gate arches, pillars and walls significant to the highest degree for 43archæology, but, viewed without the esoteric aid of this science, really not much else than a big pile of rubbish, neatly arranged, to be sure, but extremely devoid of interest; and although science and dreams were wont formerly to stand on footings exactly opposed, they had apparently here to-day come to an agreement to withdraw their aid from Norbert Hanold and deliver him over absolutely to the aimlessness of his walking and standing around.

So he had wandered in all directions from the Forum to the Amphitheatre, from the Porta di Stabia to the Porta del Vesuvio through the Street of Tombs as well as through countless others, and the sun had likewise, in the meanwhile, made its accustomed morning journey to the position where it usually changes to the more comfortable descent toward the sea. Thereby, to the great satisfaction of their misunderstood, hoarsely eloquent guides, it gave the English and American men and women, forced to go there by a traveller's sense of duty, a signal to become mindful of the superior comfort of sitting at the lunch-tables of the twin hotels; besides, they had seen with their own eyes everything that could be required for conversation on the other side of the ocean and channel; so the separate groups, satiated by the past, started on the return, ebbed in common movement down through the Via Marina, in order not to lose meals at the, to be sure somewhat euphemistically Lucullan, tables of the present, in the house of "Diomed" or of Mr. Swiss. In consideration of all the outer and inner circumstances, this was doubtless also the wisest thing that they could do, for the noon 44sun of May was decidedly well disposed toward the lizards, butterflies and other winged inhabitants or visitors of the extensive mass of ruins, but for the northern complexion of a Madame or Miss its perpendicular obtrusiveness was unquestionably beginning to become less kindly, and, supposedly in some causal connection with that, the "charmings" had already in the last hour considerably diminished, the "shockings" had increased in the same proportion, and the masculine "ah's" proceeding from rows of teeth even more widely distended than before had begun a noticeable transition to yawning.

It was remarkable, however, that simultaneously with their vanishing, what had formerly been the city of Pompeii assumed an entirely changed appearance, but not a living one; it now appeared rather to be becoming completely petrified in dead immobility. Yet out of it stirred a feeling that death was beginning to talk, although not in a manner intelligible to human ears. To be sure, here and there was a sound as if a whisper were proceeding from the stone which, however, only the softly murmuring south wind, Atabulus, awoke, he who, two thousand years ago, had buzzed in this fashion about the temples, halls and houses, and was now carrying on his playful game with the green, shimmering stalks on the low ruins. From the coast of Africa he often rushed across, casting forth wild, full blasts: he was not doing that to-day, but was gently fanning again the old acquaintances which had come to light again. He could not, however, refrain from his natural tendency to devastate, and blew with hot breath, even 45though lightly, on everything that he encountered on the way.

In this, the sun, his eternally youthful mother, helped him. She strengthened his fiery breath, and accomplished, besides, what he could not, steeped everything with trembling, glittering, dazzling splendour. As with a golden eraser, she effaced from the edges of the houses on the *semitæ* and *crepidine viarum*, as the sidewalks were once called, every slight shadow, cast into all the vestibules, inner courts, peristyles and balconies her luminous radiance, or desultory rays where a shelter blocked her direct approach. Hardly anywhere was there a nook which successfully protected itself against the ocean of light and veiled itself in a dusky, silver web; every street lay between the old walls like long, rippling, white strips of linen spread out to bleach; and without exception all were equally motionless and mute, for not only had the last of the rasping and nasal tones of the English and American messengers disappeared, but the former slight evidences of lizard- and butterfly-life seemed also to have left the silent city of ruins. They had not really done so, but the gaze perceived no more movement from them.

As had been the custom of their ancestors out on the mountain slopes and cliff walls for thousands of years, when the great Pan laid himself to sleep, here, too, in order not to disturb him, they had stretched themselves out motionless or, folding their wings, had squatted here and there; and it seemed as if, in this place, they felt even more strongly the command of the hot, holy, noonday quiet in whose ghostly hour life must be silent and 46suppressed, because during it the dead awake and begin to talk in toneless spirit-language.

This changed aspect which the things round about had assumed really thrust itself less upon the vision than it aroused the emotions, or, more correctly, an unnamed sixth sense; this latter, however, was stimulated so strongly and persistently that a person endowed with it could not throw off the effect produced upon him. To be sure, of those estimable boarders already busy with their soup spoons at the two "alberghi" near the "ingresso," hardly a man or woman would have been counted among those thus invested, but Nature had once bestowed this great attention upon Norbert Hanold and he had to submit to its effects, not at all because he had an understanding with it, however, for he wished nothing at all and desired nothing more than that he might be sitting quietly in his study with an instructive book in his hand, instead of having undertaken this aimless spring journey. Yet as he had turned back from the Street of Tombs through the Hercules gate into the centre of the city, and at Casa di Sallustio had turned to the left, quite without purpose or thought, into the narrow "vicolo," suddenly that sixth sense was awakened in him; but this last expression was not really fitting, rather he was transported by it into a strangely dreamy condition, about half-way between a waking state and loss of senses. As if guarding a secret, everywhere round about him, suffused in light, lay deathly silence, so breathless that even his own lungs hardly dared to take in air. He stood at the intersection of two streets where the Vicolo Mercurio crossed the broader 47Strada di Mercurio, which stretched out to right and left; in answer to the god of commerce, business and trades had formerly had their abodes here; the street corners spoke silently of it; many shops with broken counters, inlaid with marble, opened out upon them; here the arrangement indicated a bakery, there, a number of large, convex, earthenware jugs, an oil or flour business. Opposite more slender, two-handled jars set into the counters showed that the space behind them had been a bar-room; surely in the evening, slaves and maids of the neighbourhood might have thronged here to get wine for their masters in their own jugs; one could see that the now illegible inscription inlaid with mosaic on the sidewalk in front of the shop was worn by many feet; probably it had held out to passers-by a recommendation of the excellent wine. On the outer wall, at about half the height of a man, was visible a "graffito" probably scratched into the plastering, with his finger-nail or an iron nail, by a schoolboy, perhaps derisively explaining the praise, in this way, that the owner's wine owed its peerlessness to a generous addition of water. For from the scratch there seemed raised before Norbert Hanold's eyes the word "caupo," or was it an illusion. Certainly he could not settle it. He possessed a certain skill in deciphering "graffiti" which were difficult, and had already accomplished widely recognized work in that field, yet at this time it completely failed him. Not only that, he had a feeling that he did not understand any Latin, and it was absurd of him to wish to read what a Pompeiian school youth had scratched into the wall two thousand years before.

48Not only had all his science left him, but it left him without the least desire to regain it; he remembered it as from a great distance, and he felt that it had been an old, dried-up, boresome aunt, dullest and most superfluous creature in the world. What she uttered with puckered lips and sapient mien, and presented as wisdom, was all vain, empty pompousness, and merely gnawed at the dry rind of the fruit of knowledge without revealing anything of its content, the germ of life, or bringing anything to the point of inner, intelligent enjoyment. What it taught was a lifeless, archæological view, and what came from its mouth was a dead, philological language. These helped in no way to a comprehension with soul, mind and heart, as the saying is, but he, who possessed a desire for that, had to stand alone here, the only living person in the hot noonday silence among the remains of the past, in order not to see with physical eyes nor hear with corporeal ears. Then something came forth everywhere without movement and a soundless speech began; then the sun dissolved the tomblike rigidity of the old stones, a glowing thrill passed through them, the dead awoke, and Pompeii began to live again.

The thoughts in Norbert Hanold's mind were not really blasphemous, but he had an indefinite feeling deserving of that adjective, and with this, standing motionless, he looked before him down the Strada di Mercurio toward the city-wall. The angular lava-blocks of its pavement still lay as faultlessly fitted together as before the devastation, and each one was of a light-grey colour, yet such dazzling lustre brooded over them that they stretched like 49a

13

quilted silver-white ribbon passing in faintly glowing void between the silent walls and by the side of column fragments.

Then suddenly—

With open eyes he gazed along the street, yet it seemed to him as if he were doing it in a dream. A little to the right something suddenly stepped forth from the Casa di Castore e Polluce, and across the lava stepping-stones, which led from the house to the other side of the Strada di Mercurio, Gradiva stepped buoyantly.

Quite indubitably it was she; even if the sunbeams did surround her figure as with a thin veil of gold, he perceived her in profile as plainly and as distinctly as on the bas-relief. Her head, whose crown was entwined with a scarf which fell to her neck, inclined forward a little; her left hand held up lightly the extremely voluminous dress and, as it reached only to her ankles, one could perceive clearly that in advancing, the right foot, lingering, if only for a moment, rose on the tips of the toes almost perpendicularly. Here, however, it was not a stone representation, everything in uniform colourlessness; the dress, apparently made of extremely soft, clinging material, was not of cold marble-white, but of a warm tone verging faintly on yellow, and her hair, wavy under the scarf on her brow, and peeping forth at the temples, stood out, with golden-brown radiance, in bold contrast to her alabaster countenance.

As soon as he caught sight of her, Norbert's memory was clearly awakened to the fact that he had seen her here once already in a dream, walking thus, the night that she had lain down as if to 50sleep over there in the Forum on the steps of the Temple of Apollo. With this memory he became conscious, for the first time, of something else; he had, without himself knowing the motive in his heart, come to Italy on that account and had, without stop, continued from Rome and Naples to Pompeii to see if he could here find trace of her—and that in a literal sense—for, with her unusual gait, she must have left behind in the ashes a foot-print different from all the others.

Again it was a noonday dream-picture that passed there before him and yet also a reality. For that was apparent from an effect which it produced. On the last stepping-stone on the farther side, there lay stretched out motionless, in the burning sunlight, a big lizard, whose body, as if woven of gold and malachite, glistened brightly to Norbert's eyes. Before the approaching foot, however, it darted down suddenly and wriggled away over the white, gleaming lava pavement.

Gradiva crossed the stepping-stones with her calm buoyancy, and now, turning her back, walked along on the opposite sidewalk; her destination seemed to be the house of Adonis. Before it she stopped a moment, too, but passed then, as if after further deliberation, down farther through the Strada di Mercurio. On the left, of the more elegant buildings, there now stood only the Casa di Apollo, named after the numerous representations of Apollo excavated there, and, to the man who was gazing after her, it seemed again that she had also surely chosen the portico of the Temple of Apollo for her death sleep. Probably she was closely associated with the cult of the sun-god and was going there. 51Soon, however, she stopped again; stepping-stones crossed the street here, too, and she walked back again to the right side. Thus she turned the other side of her face toward him and looked a little different, for her left hand, which held up her gown, was not visible and instead of her curved arm, the right one hung down straight. At a greater distance now, however, the golden waves of sunlight floated around her with a thicker web of veiling, and did not allow him to distinguish where she had stopped, for she disappeared suddenly before the house of Meleager. Norbert Hanold still stood without having moved a limb. With his eyes, and this time with his corporeal ones, he had surveyed, step by step, her vanishing form. Now, at length, he drew a deep breath, for his breast too had remained almost motionless.

Simultaneously the sixth sense, suppressing the others completely, held him absolutely in its sway. Had what had just stood before him been a product of his imagination or a reality?

He did not know that, nor whether he was awake or dreaming, and tried in vain to collect his thoughts. Then, however, a strange shudder passed down his spine. He saw and heard nothing, yet he felt from the secret inner vibrations that Pompeii had begun to live about him in the noonday hour of spirits, and so Gradiva lived again, too, and had gone into the house which she had occupied before the fateful August day of the year 79.

From his former visit, he was acquainted with the Casa di Meleagro, had not yet gone there this time, however, but had merely stopped briefly in the Museo Nazionale of Naples before the wall 52paintings of Meleager and his Arcadian huntress companion, Atalanta, which had been found in the Strada di Mercurio in that house, and after which the latter had been named. Yet as he now again acquired the ability to move and walked toward it, he began to doubt whether it really bore its name after the slayer of the Caledonian boar. He suddenly recalled a Greek poet, Meleager, who, to be sure, had probably lived about a century before the destruction of Pompeii. A descendant of his, however, might have come here and built the house for himself. That agreed with something else that had awakened in his memory, for he remembered his supposition, or rather a definite conviction, that Gradiva had been of Greek descent. To be sure there mingled with his idea the figure of Atalanta as Ovid had pictured it in his*Metamorphoses*:

> —her floating vest
> A polished buckle clasped—her careless locks
> In simple knot were gathered—

Trans. by HENRY KING.

He could not recall the verses word for word, but their content was present in his mind; and from his store of knowledge was added the fact that Cleopatra was the name of the young wife of Œneus' son, Meleager. More probably this had nothing to do with him, but with the Greek poet, Meleager. Thus, under the glowing sun of the Campagna, there was a mythological-literary-historical-archæological juggling in his head.

When he had passed the house of Castor and Pollux and that of the Centaur, he stood before the Casa di Meleagro from whose threshold there 53looked up at him, still discernible, the inlaid greeting "Ave." On the wall of the vestibule, Mercury was handing Fortuna a pouch filled with money; that probably indicated, allegorically, the riches and other fortunate circumstances of the former dweller. Behind this opened up the inner court, the centre of which was occupied by a marble table supported by three griffins.

Empty and silent, the room lay there, appearing absolutely unfamiliar to the man, as he entered, awaking no memory that he had already been here, yet he then recalled it, for the interior of the house offered a deviation from that of the other excavated buildings of the city. The peristyle adjoined the inner court on the other side of the balcony toward the rear—not in the usual way, but at the left side and on that account was of greater extent and more splendid appearance than any other in Pompeii. It was framed by a colonnade supported by two dozen pillars painted red on the lower, and white on the upper half. These lent solemnity to the great, silent space; here in the centre was a spring with a beautifully wrought enclosure, which served as a fish-pool. Apparently the house must have been the dwelling of an estimable man of culture and artistic sense.

Norbert's gaze passed around, and he listened. Yet nowhere about did anything stir, nor was the slightest sound audible. Amidst this cold stone there was no longer a breath; if Gradiva had gone into Meleager's house, she had already dissolved again into nothing. At the rear of the peristyle was another room, an *œcus*, the former dining-room, likewise surrounded on three sides by pillars 54painted yellow, which shimmered from a distance in the light, as if they were encrusted with gold. Between them, however, shone a red far more dazzling than that from the walls, with which no brush of antiquity, but young Nature of the present had painted the ground. The former artistic pavement lay completely ruined, fallen to decay and weather worn; it was May which exercised here again its most ancient dominion and covered the whole *œcus*, as it did at the time in many houses of the buried city, with red, flowering, wild poppies, whose seeds the winds had carried thither, and these had sprouted in the ashes. It was a wave of densely crowded blossoms, or so it appeared, although, in reality, they stood there motionless, for Atabulus found no way down to them, but only hummed away softly above. Yet the sun cast such flaming, radiant vibrations down upon them that it gave an impression of red ripples in a pond undulating hither and thither. Norbert Hanold's eyes had passed unheeding over a similar sight in other houses, but here he was strangely thrilled by it. The dream-flower grown at the edge of Lethe filled the space, and Hypnos lay stretched in their midst dispensing sleep, which dulls the senses, with the saps which night has gathered in the red chalices. It seemed to the man who had entered the dining-room through the portico of the peristyle as if he felt his temples touched by the invisible slumber wand of the old vanquisher of gods and men, but not with heavy stupor; only a dreamily sweet loveliness floated about his consciousness. At the same time, however, he still remained in control of his feet and stepped along by the wall 55of the former dining-room from which gazed old pictures: Paris, awarding the apple; a satyr, carrying in his hand an asp and tormenting a young Bacchante with it.

But there again suddenly, unforeseen—only about five paces away from him—in the narrow shadow cast down by a single piece of the upper part of the dining-room portico, which still remained in a state of preservation, sitting on the low steps between two of the yellow pillars was a brightly clad woman who now raised her head. In that way she disclosed to the unnoticed arrival, whose footstep she had apparently just heard, a full view of her face, which produced in him a double feeling, for it appeared to him at the same time unknown and yet also familiar, already seen or imagined; but by his arrested breathing and his heart palpitations, he recognized, unmistakably, to whom it belonged. He had found what he was looking for, what had driven him unconsciously to Pompeii; Gradiva continued her visible existence in the noonday spirit hour and sat here before him as, in the dream, he had seen her on the steps of the Temple of Apollo. Spread out on her knees lay something white, which he was unable to distinguish clearly; it seemed to be a papyrus sheet, and a red poppy-blossom stood out from it in marked contrast.

In her face surprise was expressed; under the lustrous, brown hair and the beautiful, alabaster brow, two rarely bright, starlike eyes looked at him with questioning amazement. It required only a few moments for him to recognize the conformity of her features with those of the profile. They must be thus, viewed from the front, and therefore, at 56first glance, they had not been really unfamiliar to him. Near to, her white dress, by its slight tendency to yellow, heightened still more the warm colour; apparently it consisted of a fine, extremely soft, woollen material, which produced abundant folds, and the scarf around her head was of the same. Below, on the nape of the neck, appeared again the shimmering, brown hair artlessly gathered in a single knot; at her throat, under a dainty chin, a little gold clasp held her gown together.

Norbert Hanold dimly perceived that involuntarily he had raised his hand to his soft Panama hat and removed it; and now he said in Greek, "Are you Atalanta, the daughter of Jason, or are you a descendant of the family of the poet, Meleager?"

Without giving an answer, the lady addressed looked at him silently with a calmly wise expression in her eyes, and two thoughts passed through his mind; either her resurrected self could not speak, or she was not of Greek descent and was ignorant of the language. He therefore substituted Latin for it and asked: "Was your father a distinguished Pompeiian citizen of Latin origin?"

To this she was equally silent, only about her delicately curved lips there was a slight quiver as if she were repressing a burst of laughter. Now a feeling of fright came upon him; apparently she was sitting there before him like a silent image, a phantom to whom speech was denied. Consternation at this discovery was stamped fully and distinctly upon his features.

Then, however, her lips could no longer resist the impulse; a real smile played about them and 57at the same time a voice sounded from between them, "If you wish to speak with me, you must do so in German."

That was really remarkable from the mouth of a Pompeiian woman who had died two centuries before, or would have been so for a person hearing it in a different state of mind. Yet every oddity escaped Norbert because of two waves of emotion which had rushed over him, one because Gradiva possessed the power of speech, and the other was one which had been forced from his inmost being by her voice. It sounded as clear as was her glance; not sharp, but reminiscent of the tones of a bell, her voice passed through the sunny silence over the blooming poppy-field, and the young archæologist suddenly realized that he had already

16

heard it thus in his imagination, and involuntarily he gave audible expression to his feeling, "I knew that your voice sounded like that."

One could read in her countenance that she was seeking comprehension of something, but was not finding it. To his last remark she now responded, "How could you? You have never talked with me."

To him it was not at all remarkable that she spoke German, and, according to present usage, addressed him formally; as she did it, he understood completely that it could not have happened otherwise, and he answered quickly, "No—not talked—but I called to you when you lay down to sleep and stood near you then—your face was as calmly beautiful as if it were of marble. May I beg you—rest it again on the step in that way."

While he was speaking, something peculiar had 58occurred. A golden butterfly, faintly tinged with red on the inner edge of its upper wing, fluttered from the poppies toward the pillars, flitted a few times about Gradiva's head and then rested on the brown, wavy hair above her brow. At the same time, however, she rose, slender and tall, for she stood up with deliberate haste, curtly and silently directed at Norbert another glance, in which something suggested that she considered him demented; then, thrusting her foot forward, she walked out in her characteristic way along the pillars of the old portico. Only fleetingly visible for a while, she finally seemed to have sunk into the earth.

He stood up, breathless, as if stunned; yet with heavy understanding he had grasped what had occurred before his eyes. The noonday ghost hour was over, and in the form of a butterfly, a winged messenger had come up from the asphodel meadows of Hades to admonish the departed one to return. For him something else was associated with this, although in confused indistinctness. He knew that the beautiful butterfly of Mediterranean countries bore the name Cleopatra, and this had also been the name of Caledonian Meleager's young wife who, in grief over his death, had given herself as sacrifice to those of the lower world.

From his mouth issued a call to the girl who was departing, "Are you coming here again to-morrow in the noon hour?" Yet she did not turn around, gave no answer, and disappeared after a few moments in the corner of the dining-room behind the pillar. Now a compelling impulse suddenly incited him to hasten after her, but her 59bright dress was no longer visible anywhere; glowing with the hot sun's rays, the Casa di Meleagro lay about him motionless and silent; only Cleopatra hovered on her red, shimmering, golden wings, making slow circles again above the multitude of poppies.

When and how he had returned to the "ingresso," Norbert Hanold could not recall; in his memory he retained only the idea that his appetite had peremptorily demanded to be appeased, though very tardily, at the "Diomed," and then he had wandered forth aimlessly on the first good street, had arrived at the beach north of Castellamare, where he had seated himself on a lava-block, and the sea-wind had blown around his head until the sun had set about half-way between Monte Sant' Angelo above Sorrento and Monte Epomeo on Ischia. Yet, in spite of this stay of at least several hours by the water, he had obtained from the fresh air there no mental relief, but was returning to the hotel in the same condition in which he had left it. He found the other guests busily occupied with dinner, had a little bottle of Vesuvio wine brought to him in a corner of the room, viewed the faces of those eating, and listened to their conversations. From the faces of all, as well as from their talk, it appeared to him absolutely certain that in the noon hour none of them had either met or spoken to a dead Pompeiian woman who had returned again briefly to life. Of course, all this had been a foregone conclusion, as they had all been at lunch at that time; why and 60wherefore, he himself could not state, yet after a while he went over to the competitor of the "Diomed," "Hotel Suisse," sat down there also in a corner, and, as he had to order something, likewise before a little bottle of Vesuvio, and here he gave himself over to the same kind of investigations with eye and ear. They led to the same results but also to the further conclusion that he now knew by sight all the temporary, living visitors of Pompeii. To be sure, this effected an increase of his knowledge which he could hardly consider an enrichment, but from it he experienced a certain satisfying feeling that, in the two hostelries, no guest, either male or female, was present with whom, by means of sight and hearing, he

17

had not entered into a personal, even if one-sided, relation. Of course, in no way had the absurd supposition entered his mind that he might possibly meet Gradiva in one of the two hotels, but he could have taken his oath that no one was staying in them who possessed, in the remotest way, any trace of resemblance to her. During his observations, he had occasionally poured wine from his little bottle to his glass, and had drunk from time to time; and when, in this manner, the former had gradually become empty, he rose and went back to the "Diomed." The heavens were now strewn with countless, flashing, twinkling, stars, but not in the traditionally stationary way, for Norbert gathered the impression that Perseus, Cassiopeia and Andromeda with some neighbours, bowing lightly hither and thither, were performing a singing dance, and below, on earth, too, it seemed to him that the dark shadows of the tree-tops and buildings did not stay in the same place. Of course on the ground of this region—unsteady from ancient times—this could not be exactly surprising, for the subterranean glow lurked everywhere, after an eruption, and let a little of itself rise in the vines and grapes from which was pressed Vesuvio, which was not one of Norbert Hanold's usual evening drinks. He still remembered, however, even if a little of the circular movement of things might be ascribed to the wine, too, that since noon all objects had displayed an inclination to whirl softly about his head, and therefore he found, in the slight increase, nothing new, but only a continuation of the formerly existing conditions. He went up to his room and stood for a little while at the open window, looking over toward the Vesuvius mound, above which now no cone of smoke spread its top, but rather something like the fluctuations of a dark, purple cloak flowed back and forth around it. Then the young archæologist undressed, without having lighted the light, and sought his couch. Yet, as he stretched himself out upon it, it was not his bed at the "Diomed," but a red poppy-field whose blossoms closed over him like a soft cushion heated by the sun. His enemy, the common house-fly, constrained by darkness to lethargic stupidity, sat fiftyfold above his head, on the wall, and only one moved, even in its sleepiness, by desire to torture, buzzed about his nose. He recognized it, however, not as the absolute evil, the century-old scourge of humanity, for before his eyes it poised like a red-gold Cleopatra.

When, in the morning, the sun, with lively assistance from the flies, awoke him, he could not recall what, besides strange, Ovid-like metamorphoses, had occurred during the night about his bed. Yet doubtless some mystic being, continuously weaving dream-webs, had been sitting beside him, for he felt his head completely overhung and filled with them, so that all ability to think lay inextricably imprisoned in it and only one thing remained in his consciousness; he must again be in Meleager's house at exactly noon. In this connection, however, a fear overcame him, for if the gatekeepers at the "ingresso" looked at him, they would not let him in. Anyway it was not advisable that he should expose himself to close observation by human eyes. To escape that, there was, for one well informed about Pompeii, a means which was, to be sure, against the rules, but he was not in a condition to grant to legal regulation a determination of his conduct. So he climbed again, as on the evening of his arrival, along the old city-wall, and upon it walked, in a wide semicircle, around the city of ruins to the solitary, unguarded Porta di Nola. Here it was not difficult to get down into the inside and he went, without burdening his conscience very much over the fact that by his autocratic deed he had deprived the administration of a two-lira entrance fee, which he could, of course, let it have later in some other way.

Thus, unseen, he had reached an uninteresting part of the city, never before investigated by any one and still mostly unexcavated; he sat down in a secluded, shady nook and waited, now and then drawing his watch to observe the progress of time. Once his glance fell upon something in the distance gleaming, silvery-white, rising from the ashes, but with his unreliable vision, he was unable to distinguish what it was. Yet involuntarily he was impelled to go up to it and there it stood, a tall, flowering asphodel-plant with white, bell-like blossoms whose seeds the wind had carried thither from outside. It was the flower of the lower world, significant and, as he felt, destined to grow here for his purpose. He broke the slender stem and returned with it to his seat. Hotter and hotter the May sun burned down as on the day before, and finally approached its noonday position; so now he started out through the long Strada di Nola. This lay deathly still and deserted, as did almost all the others; over there to the west all the morning visitors were already crowding again to the Porta Marina and the soup-plates. Only the air, suffused with heat, stirred, and in the dazzling glare the solitary figure of Norbert Hanold with the asphodel branch appeared like that of Hermes, Psyche's escort, in modern attire, starting out upon the journey to conduct a departed soul to Hades.

Not consciously, yet following an instinctive impulse, he found his way through the Strada della Fortuna farther along to the Strada di Mercurio, and turning to the right arrived at the Casa di Meleagro. Just as lifelessly as yesterday, the vestibule, inner court and peristyle received him, and between the pillars of the latter the poppies of the dining-room flamed across to him. As he entered, however, it was not clear to him whether he had been here yesterday or two thousand years ago to seek from the owner of the house some information of great importance to archæology; what it was, however, he could not state, and besides, it seemed to him, even though in contradiction to the above, that all the science of antiquity was the most purposeless and indifferent thing in the world. He could not understand how a human being could occupy himself with it, for there was only a single thing to which all thinking and investigation must be directed: what is the nature of the physical manifestation of a being like Gradiva, dead and alive at the same time, although the latter was true only in the noon hour of spirits—or had been the day before, perhaps the one time in a century or a thousand years, for it suddenly seemed certain that his return to-day was in vain. He did not meet the girl he was looking for, because she was not allowed to come again until a time when he too would have been dead for many years, and was buried and forgotten. Of course, as he walked now along by the wall below Paris awarding the apple, he perceived Gradiva before him, just as on yesterday, in the same gown, sitting between the same two yellow pillars on the same step. Yet he did not allow himself to be deceived by tricks of imagination, but knew that fancy alone was deceptively depicting before his eyes what he had really seen there the day before. He could not refrain, however, from stopping to indulge in the view of the shadowy apparition created by himself and, without his knowing it, there passed from his lips in a grieved tone the words, "Oh, that you were still alive!"

His voice rang out, but, after that, breathless silence again reigned among the ruins of the old dining-room. Yet soon another sounded through the vacant stillness, saying, "Won't you sit down too? You look exhausted."

Norbert Hanold's heart stood still a moment. His head, however, collected this much reason; a vision could not speak; or was an aural hallucination practising deception upon him? With fixed gaze, he supported himself against the pillar.

Then again asked the voice, and it was the one which none other than Gradiva possessed, "Are you bringing me the white flowers?"

Dizziness rushed upon him; he felt that his feet no longer supported him, but forced him to be seated; and he slid down opposite her on the step, against the pillar. Her bright eyes were directed toward his face, yet with a different look from the one with which she had gazed at him yesterday when she suddenly rose and went away. In that, something ill-humoured and repellent had spoken; but it had disappeared, as if she had, in the meanwhile, arrived at a different view-point, and an expression of searching inquisitiveness or curiosity had taken its place. Likewise, she spoke with an easy familiarity. As he remained silent, however, to the last question also, she again resumed, "You told me yesterday that you had once called to me when I lay down to sleep and that you had afterwards stood near me; my face was as white as marble. When and where was that? I cannot remember it, and I beg you to explain more exactly."

Norbert had now acquired enough power of speech to answer, "In the night when you sat on the steps of the Temple of Apollo in the Forum and the fall of ashes from Vesuvius covered you."

"So—then. Yes, to be sure—that had not occurred to me, but I might have thought that it would be a case like that. When you said it yesterday, I was not expecting it, and I was utterly unprepared. Yet that happened, if I recall correctly, two thousand years ago. Were you living then? It seems to me you look younger." She spoke very seriously, but at the end a faint, extremely sweet smile played about her mouth. He hesitated in embarrassment and answered, stuttering slightly, "No, I really don't believe I was alive in the year 79—it was perhaps—yes, it surely is a psychic condition which is called a dream that transported me into the time of the destruction of Pompeii—but I recognized you again at first glance."

In the expression of the girl sitting opposite him, a few feet away, surprise was apparent, and she repeated in a tone of amazement, "You recognized me again? In the dream? By what?"

"At the very first; by your manner of walking."

"Had you noticed that? And have I a special manner of walking?"

Her astonishment had grown perceptibly. He replied, "Yes—don't you realize that? A more graceful one—at least among those now living—does not exist. Yet I recognized you immediately by everything else too, your figure, face, bearing and drapery, for everything agreed most minutely with the bas-relief of you in Rome."

"Ah, really—" she repeated in her former tone—"with the bas-relief of me in Rome. Yes, I hadn't thought of that either, and at this moment 67I don't know exactly—what is it—and you saw it there then?"

Now he told her that the sight of it had attracted him so that he had been highly pleased to get a plaster-cast of it in Germany, and that for years it had hung in his room. He observed it daily, and the idea had come to him that it must represent a young Pompeiian girl who was walking on the stepping-stones of a street in her native city; and the dream had confirmed it. Now he knew also that he had been impelled by it to travel here again to see whether he could find some trace of her; and as he had stood yesterday noon at the corner of Strada di Mercurio, she, herself, exactly like her image, had suddenly walked before him across the stepping-stones, as if she were about to go over into the house of Apollo. Then farther along she had recrossed the street and disappeared before the house of Meleager.

To this she nodded and said, "Yes, I intended to look up the house of Apollo, but I came here."

He continued, "On that account the Greek poet, Meleager, came to my mind, and I thought that you were one of his descendants and were returning—in the hour which you are allowed—to your ancestral home. When I spoke to you in Greek, however, you did not understand."

"Was that Greek? No, I don't understand it or I've probably forgotten it. Yet as you came again just now, I heard you say something that I could understand. You expressed the wish that some one might still be alive here. Only I did not understand whom you meant by that."

That caused him to reply that, at sight of her, 68he had believed that it was not really she, but that his imagination was deceptively putting her image before him in the place where he had met her yesterday. At that she smiled and agreed, "It seems that you have reason to be on your guard against an excess of imagination, although, when I have been with you, I never supposed so." She stopped, however, and added, "What is there peculiar about my way of walking, which you spoke of before?"

It was noteworthy that her aroused interest brought her back to that, and he said, "If I may ask——"

With that he stopped, for he suddenly remembered with fear that yesterday she had suddenly risen and gone away when he had asked her to lie down to sleep again on that step, as on that of the Temple of Apollo, and, associated darkly with this, there came to him the glance which she had directed upon him in departing. Yet now the calm, friendly expression of her eyes remained, and as he spoke no further, she said, "It was nice that your wish that some one might still be alive concerned me. If you wish to ask anything of me on that account, I will gladly respond."

That overcame his fear, and he replied, "It would make me happy to get a close view of you walking as you do in the bas-relief."

Willingly, without answering, she stood up and walked along between the wall and the pillars. It was the very buoyantly reposeful gait, with the sole raised almost perpendicularly, that was so firmly imprinted on his mind, but for the first time he saw that she wore, below the raised gown, not 69sandals, but light, sand-coloured shoes of fine leather. When she came back and sat down again silently, he involuntarily started to talk of the difference in her foot-covering from that of the bas-relief. To that she rejoined, "Time, of course, always changes everything, and for the present sandals are not suitable, so I put on shoes, which are a better protection against rain and dust; but why did you ask me to walk before you? What is there peculiar about it?"

Her repeated wish to learn this proved her not entirely free from feminine curiosity. He now explained that it was a matter of the peculiarly upright position of the rising foot, as she walked, and he added how for weeks he had tried to observe the gait of modern women on the streets in his native city. Yet it seemed that this beautiful way of walking had been completely lost to them, with the exception, perhaps, of a single one who had given him the impression that she walked in that way. To be sure, he had not been able to establish this fact because of the crowd about her, and he had probably experienced an illusion, for it had seemed to him that her features had resembled somewhat those of Gradiva.

"What a shame," she answered. "For confirmation of the fact would surely have been of great scientific importance, and if you had succeeded, perhaps you would not have needed to take the long journey here; but whom were you just speaking of? Who is Gradiva?"

"I have named the bas-relief that, because I didn't know your real name, and don't know it yet, either."

70This last he added with some hesitancy, and she faltered a moment before replying to the indirect question. "My name is Zoë."

With pained tone the words escaped him: "The name suits you beautifully, but it sounds to me like bitter mockery, for 'Zoë' means 'life.'"

"One must adapt himself to the inevitable," she responded, "and I have long accustomed myself to being dead; but now my time is over for to-day; you have brought the grave-flower with you to conduct me back. So give it to me."

As she rose and stretched forth her slender hand, he gave her the asphodel cluster, but was careful not to touch her fingers. Accepting the flowering branch she said, "I thank you. To those who are more fortunate one gives roses in spring, but for me the flower of oblivion is the right one from your hand. To-morrow I shall be allowed to come here again at this hour. If your way leads you again into the house of Meleager, we can sit together at the edge of the poppies, as we did to-day. On the threshold stands 'Ave,' and I say it to you 'Ave'!"

She went out and disappeared, as yesterday, at the turn in the portico, as if she had there sunk into the ground. Everything lay empty and silent again, but, from some distance, there once rang, short and clear, a sound like the merry note of a bird flying over the devastated city. This was stifled immediately, however. Norbert, who had remained behind, looked down at the step where she had just been sitting; there something white shimmered; it seemed to be the papyrus leaf which Gradiva had held on her knees yesterday and had 71forgotten to take with her to-day. Yet, as he shyly reached for it, he found it to be a little sketch-book with pencil drawings of the different ruins in several houses of Pompeii. The page next to the last showed a drawing of the griffin-table in the central court of the Casa di Meleagro, and on the last was the beginning of a reproduction of the view across the poppies of the dining-room through the row of pillars of the peristyle. That the departed girl made drawings in a sketch-book of the present mode was as amazing as had been the fact that she expressed her thoughts in German. Yet those were only insignificant prodigies beside the great one of her revivification, and apparently she used the midday hour of freedom to preserve for herself, in their present state, with unusual artistic talent, the surroundings in which she had once lived. The drawings testified to delicately cultivated powers of perception, as each of her words did to a clever intellect; and she had probably often sat by the old griffin-table, so that it was a particularly precious reminder.

Mechanically Norbert also went, with the little book, along the portico, and at the place where this turned he noticed in the wall a narrow cleft wide enough to afford, to an unusually slender figure, passage into the adjoining building, and even farther to the Vicolo del Fauno at the other side of the house. Suddenly, however, the idea flashed through his mind that Zoë-Gradiva did not sink into the ground here—that was essentially unreasonable, and he could not understand how he had ever believed it—but went, on this street, back to her tomb. That must be in the Street of Tombs, 72and rushing forth, he hastened out into the Strada di Mercurio and as far as the gate of Hercules; but when, breathless and reeking with perspiration, he entered this, it was already too late. The broad Strada di Sepolcri stretched out empty and dazzlingly white, only at its extremity, behind the glimmering curtain of radiance, a faint shadow seemed to dissolve uncertainly before the Villa of Diomede.

Norbert Hanold passed the second half of the day with a feeling that Pompeii was everywhere, or at least wherever he stopped, veiled in a cloud of mist. It was not grey, gloomy and melancholy as formerly, but rather cheerful and vari-coloured to an extraordinary degree; blue, red and brown, chiefly a light-yellowish white and alabaster white, interwoven with golden threads of sunbeams. This injured neither his power of vision nor that of hearing, only, because of it, thinking was impossible, and that produced a cloud-wall whose effect rivalled the thickest mist. To the young archæologist it seemed almost as if hourly, in an invisible and not otherwise noticeable way, there was brought to him a little bottle of Vesuvio wine, which produced a continuous whirling in his head. From this he instinctively sought to free himself by the use of correctives, on the one hand drinking water frequently, and on the other hand moving about as much and as far as possible. His knowledge of medicine was not comprehensive, but it helped him to the diagnosis that this strange condition must arise from excessive congestion of blood in his 73head, perhaps associated with accelerated action of the heart; for he felt the latter—something formerly quite unknown to him—occasionally beating fast against his chest. Otherwise, his thoughts, which could not penetrate into the outer world, were not in the least inactive within, or more exactly, there was only one thought there, which had come into sole possession and carried on a restless, though vain activity. It continually turned about the question of what physical nature Zoë-Gradiva might possess, whether during her stay in the house of Meleager she was a corporeal being or only an illusory representation of what she had formerly been. For the former, physical, physiological and anatomical facts seemed to argue that she had at her disposal organs of speech, and could hold a pencil with her fingers. Yet Norbert was overwhelmed with the idea that if he should touch her, even lightly place his hand on hers, he would then encounter only empty air. A peculiar impulse urged him to make sure of this, but an equally great timidity hindered him from even thinking of doing it. For he felt that the confirmation of either of the two possibilities must bring with it something inspiring fear. The corporeal existence of the hand would thrill him with horror, and its lack of substance would cause him deep pain.

Occupied vainly with this problem, which was impossible to solve scientifically without experiment, he arrived, in the course of his extensive wanderings that afternoon, at the foothills of the big mountain group of Monte Sant' Angelo, rising south from Pompeii, and here he unexpectedly came upon an elderly man, already grey-bearded, 74who, from his equipment with all sorts of implements, seemed to be a zoologist or botanist, and appeared to be making a search on a hot, sunny slope. He turned his head as Norbert came close to him, looked at the latter in surprise for a moment and then said, "Are you interested in *Faraglionensis*? I should hardly have supposed it, but it seems thoroughly probable that they are found, not only in the *Faraglioni* of Capri, but also dwell permanently on the mainland. The method suggested by my colleague, Eimer, is really good; I have already used it often with the best of success. Please remain quite still——"

The speaker stopped, stepped carefully forward a few paces and, stretched out motionless on the ground, held a little snare, made of a long grass-blade, before a narrow crevice in the rock, from which the blue, chatoyant little head of a lizard peeped. Thus the man remained without the slightest movement, and Norbert Hanold turned about noiselessly behind him and returned by the way he had come. It seemed to him dimly that he had already seen the face of the lizard-hunter once, probably in one of the two hotels; to this fact the latter's manner pointed. It was hardly credible what foolishly remarkable purposes could cause people to make the long trip to Pompeii; happy that he had succeeded in so quickly ridding himself of the snare-layer, and being again able to direct his thoughts to the problem of corporeal reality or unreality, he started on the return. Yet a side street misled him once to a wrong turn and took him, instead of to the west boundary, to the east end of the extensive old city-wall; buried 75in thought, he did not notice the mistake until he had come right up to a building which was neither the "Diomed" nor the "Hotel Suisse." In spite of this it bore the sign of an hotel; near by he recognized the ruins of the large Pompeiian amphitheatre, and the memory came to him that near this latter there was another hotel, the "Albergo del Sole," which, on account of its remoteness from the station, was sought out by only a few guests, and had remained unknown to even him. The walk had made him hot; besides, the cloudy whirling in his head had not diminished; so he stepped in through the open door and ordered the remedy deemed useful by him for blood congestion, a bottle of lime-water. The room stood empty except, of course, for the fly-visitors gathered in full numbers, and the unoccupied host availed himself of the opportunity to recommend highly his house and the excavated treasures it contained. He pointed suggestively to the fact that there were, near Pompeii, people at whose places there was not a single genuine piece among the many objects offered for sale, but that all were imitations, while he, satisfying himself with a smaller number, offered his guests only things undoubtedly genuine. For he acquired no articles which he himself had not seen brought to the light of day, and, in the course of his eloquence, he revealed that he had also been present when they had found near the Forum the young lovers who had clasped each other in firm embrace when they realized their inevitable destruction, and had thus awaited death. Norbert had already heard of this discovery, but had shrugged his shoulders about it as a fabulous invention of [76]some especially imaginative narrator, and he did so now, too, when the host brought in to him, as authentic proof, a metal brooch encrusted with green patina, which, in his presence, had been gathered with the remains of the girl from the ashes. When the arrival at the "Sun Hotel" took it in his own hand, however, the power of imagination exercised such ascendency over him that suddenly, without further critical consideration, he paid for it the price asked from English people, and, with his acquisition, hastily left the "Albergo del Sole," in which, after another turn, he saw in an open window, nodding down, an asphodel branch covered with white blossoms, which had been placed in a water-glass; and without needing any logical connection, it rushed through his mind, at the sight of the grave-flower, that it was an attestation of the genuineness of his new possession.

This he viewed with mingled feelings of excitement and shyness, keeping now to the way along the city-wall to Porta Marina. Then it was no fairy tale that a couple of young lovers had been excavated near the Forum in such an embrace, and there at the Apollo temple he had seen Gradiva lie down to sleep, but only in a dream; that he knew now quite definitely; in reality she might have gone on still farther from the Forum, met some one and died with him.

From the green brooch between his fingers a feeling passed through him that it had belonged to Zoë-Gradiva, and had held her dress closed at the throat. Then she was the beloved fiancée, perhaps the young wife of him with whom she had wished to die.

[77]It occurred to Norbert Hanold to hurl the brooch away. It burned his fingers as if it had become glowing, or more exactly, it caused him the pain such as he had felt at the idea that he might put his hand on that of Gradiva and encounter only empty air.

Reason, nevertheless, asserted the upper hand; he did not allow himself to be controlled by imagination against his will. However probable it might be, there was still lacking invincible proof that the brooch had belonged to her and that it had been she who had been discovered in the young man's arms. This judgment made it possible for him to breathe freely, and when at the dawn of twilight he reached the "Diomed," his long wandering had brought to his sound constitution need of physical refreshment. Not without appetite did he devour the rather Spartan evening meal which the "Diomed," in spite of its Argive origin, had adopted, and he then noticed two guests newly-arrived in the course of the afternoon. By appearance and language they marked themselves as Germans, a man and a woman; they both had youthful, attractive features endowed with intellectual expressions; their relation to each other could not be determined, yet, because of a certain resemblance, Norbert decided that they were brother and sister. To be sure the young man's fair hair differed in colour from her light-brown tresses. In her gown she wore a red Sorrento rose, the sight of which, as he looked across from his corner, stirred something in his memory without his being able to think what it was. The couple were the first people he had met on his journey who seemed possibly congenial. [78]They talked with one another, over a little bottle, in not too plainly audible tones, nor in cautious whisperings, apparently sometimes about serious things and sometimes about gay things, for at times there passed over her face a half-laughing expression which was very becoming to her, and aroused the desire to participate in their conversation, or perhaps might have awakened it in Norbert, if he had met them two days before in the room otherwise populated only by Anglo-Americans. Yet he felt that what was passing through his mind stood in too strong contrast to the happy naïveté of the couple about whom there undeniably lay not the slightest cloud, for they doubtless were not meditating profoundly over the essential nature of a girl who had died two thousand years ago, but, without any weariness, were taking pleasure in an enigmatical problem of their life of the present. His condition did not harmonize with that; on the one hand he seemed superfluous to them, and on the other, he recoiled from an attempt to start an acquaintance with them, for he had a dark feeling that their bright, merry eyes might look through his forehead into his thoughts and thereby assume an expression as if they did not consider him quite in his right mind. Therefore he went up to his room, stood, as yesterday, at the window, looking over to the purple night-mantle of Vesuvius, and then he lay down to rest. Exhausted, he soon fell asleep and dreamed, but remarkably nonsensically. Somewhere in the sun Gradiva sat making a trap out of a blade of grass in order to catch a lizard, and she said, "Please stay quite still—my colleague is right; the method is really good, and she has used it with the greatest success."

Norbert Hanold became conscious in his dream that it was actually the most utter madness, and he cast about to free himself from it. He succeeded in this by the aid of an invisible bird, who seemingly uttered a short, merry call, and carried the lizard away in its beak; afterwards everything disappeared.

On awakening he remembered that in the night a voice had said that in the spring one gave roses, or rather this was recalled to him through his eyes, for his gaze, passing down from the window, came upon a bright bush of red flowers. They were of the same kind as those which the young lady had worn in her bosom, and when he went down he involuntarily plucked a couple and smelled of them. In fact, there must be something peculiar about Sorrento roses, for their fragrance seemed to him not only wonderful, but quite new and unfamiliar, and at the same time he felt that they had a somewhat liberating effect upon his mind. At least they freed him from yesterday's timidity before the gatekeepers, for he went, according to directions, in through the "ingresso" to Pompeii, paid double the amount of admission fee, and quickly struck out upon streets which took him from the vicinity of other visitors. The little sketch-book from the house of Meleager he carried along with the green brooch and the red roses, but the fragrance of the latter had made him forget to eat breakfast, and his thoughts were not in the present, but were directed exclusively to the noon hour, which was still far off; he had to pass the remaining interval, and for this purpose he entered now one house, now another, as a result of which activity the idea probably occurred to him that Gradiva had also walked there often before or even now sought these places out sometimes—his supposition that she was able to do it only at noon was tottering. Perhaps she was at liberty to do it in other hours of the day, possibly even at night in the moonlight. The roses strengthened this supposition strangely for him, when he inhaled, as he held them to his nose; and his deliberations, complaisant, and open to conviction, made advances to this new idea, for he could bear witness that he did not cling to preconceived opinions at all, but rather gave free rein to every reasonable objection, and such there was here without any doubt, not only logically, but desirably valid. Only the question arose whether, upon meeting her then, the eyes of others could see her as a corporeal being, or whether only his possessed the ability to do that. The former was not to be denied, claimed even probability for itself, transformed the desirable thing into quite the opposite, and transported him into a low-spirited, restless mood. The thought that others might also speak to her and sit down near her to carry on a conversation with her made him indignant; to that he alone possessed a claim, or at any rate a privilege, for he had discovered Gradiva, of whom no one had formerly known, had observed her daily, taken her into his life, to a degree, imparted to her his life-strength, and it seemed to him as if he had thereby again lent to her life that she would not have possessed without him. Therefore he felt that there devolved upon him a right, to which he alone might make a claim, and which he might refuse to share with anyone else.

The advancing day was hotter than the two preceding; the sun seemed to have set her mind to-day on a quite extraordinary feat, and made it regrettable, not only in an archæological, but also in a practical connection, that the water system of Pompeii had lain burst and dried up for two thousand years. Street fountains here and there commemorated it and likewise gave evidence of their informal use by thirsty passers-by, who had, in order to bend forward to the jet, leaned a hand on the marble railing and gradually dug out a sort of trough in the place, in the same way that dropping wears away stone; Norbert observed this at a corner of the Strada della Fortuna, and from that the idea occurred to him that the hand of Zoë-Gradiva, too, might formerly have rested here in that way, and involuntarily he laid his hand into the little hollow, yet he immediately rejected the idea, and felt annoyance at himself that he could have done it; the thought did not harmonize at all with the nature and bearing of the young Pompeiian girl of a refined family; there was something profane in the idea that she could have bent over so and placed her lips on the very pipe from which the plebeians drank with coarse mouths. In a noble sense, he had never seen anything more seemly than her actions and movements; he was frightened by the idea that she might be able to see by looking at him that he had had the incredibly unreasonable thought, for her eyes possessed something penetrating; a couple of times, when he had been with her, the feeling had seized him that she looked as if she were seeking for access to his inmost thoughts and were looking about them as if with a bright steel probe. He was obliged, therefore, to take great care that she might come upon nothing foolish in his mental processes.

It was now an hour until noon and in order to pass it, he went diagonally across the street into the Casa del Fauno, the most extensive and magnificent of all the excavated houses. Like no other, it possessed a double inner court and showed, in the larger one, on the middle of the ground, the empty base on which had stood the famous statue of the dancing faun after which the house had been named. Yet there stirred in Norbert Hanold not the least regret that this work of art, valued highly by science, was no longer here, but, together with the mosaic picture of the Battle of Alexander, had been transferred to the Museo Nazionale in Naples; he possessed no further intention nor desire than to let time move along, and he wandered about aimlessly in this place through the large building. Behind the peristyle opened a wider room, surrounded by numerous pillars, planned either as another repetition of the peristyle or as an ornamental garden; so it seemed at present for, like the dining-room of the Casa di Meleagro, it was completely covered with poppy-blooms. Absent-mindedly the visitor passed through the silent dereliction.

Then, however, he stopped and rested on one foot; but he found himself not alone here; at some distance his glance fell upon two figures, who first gave the impression of only one, because they stood as close as possible to each other. They did not see him, for they were concerned only with themselves, and, in that corner, because of the pillars, might have believed themselves undiscoverable by any other eyes. Mutually embracing each other, they held their lips also pressed together, and the unsuspected spectator recognized, to his amazement, that they were the young man and woman who had last evening seemed to him the first congenial people encountered on this trip. For brother and sister, their present position, the embrace and the kiss, it seemed to him had lasted too long. So it was surely another pair of lovers, probably a young bridal couple, an Augustus and Gretchen, too.

Strange to relate, however, the two latter did not, at the moment, enter Norbert's mind, and the incident seemed to him not at all ridiculous nor repulsive, rather it heightened his pleasure in them. What they were doing seemed to him as natural as it did comprehensible; his eyes clung to the living picture, more widely open than they ever had been to any of the most admired works of art, and he would have gladly devoted himself for a longer time to his observation. Yet it seemed to him that he had wrongfully penetrated into a consecrated place and was on the point of disturbing a secret act of devotion; the idea of being noticed there struck terror to his heart, and he quickly turned, went back some distance noiselessly on tiptoe and, when he had passed beyond hearing distance, ran out with bated breath and beating heart to the Vicolo del Fauno.

When he arrived before the house of Meleager, he did not know whether it was already noon, and did not happen to question his watch about it, but remained before the door, standing looking down with indecision for some time at the "Ave" in the entrance. A fear prevented him from stepping in, and strangely, he was equally afraid of not meeting Gradiva within, and of finding her there; for, during the last few moments, he had felt quite sure that, in the first case, she would be staying somewhere else with some younger man, and, in the second case, the latter would be in company with her on the steps between the pillars. Toward the man, however, he felt a hate far stronger than against all the assembled common house-flies; until to-day he had not considered it possible that he could be capable of such violent inner excitement. The duel, which he had always considered stupid nonsense, suddenly appeared to him in a different light; here it became a natural right which the man injured in his own rights, or mortally insulted, made use of as the only available means to secure satisfaction or to part with an existence which had become purposeless. So he suddenly stepped forward to enter; he would challenge the bold man and would—this rushed upon him almost more powerfully—express unreservedly to her that he had considered her something better, more noble, and incapable of such vulgarity.

He was so filled to the brim with this rebellious idea that he uttered it, even though there was not apparently the least occasion for it, for, when he had covered the distance to the dining-room with stormy haste, he demanded violently, "Are you 85alone?" although appearances allowed of no doubt that Gradiva was sitting there on the steps, just as much alone as on the two previous days.

She looked at him amazed and replied, "Who should still be here after noon? Then the people are all hungry and sit down to meals. Nature has arranged that very happily for me."

His surging excitement could not, however, be allayed so quickly, and without his knowledge or desire, he let slip, with the conviction of certainty, the conjecture which had come over him outside; for he added, to be sure somewhat foolishly, that he could really not think otherwise.

Her bright eyes remained fixed upon his face until he had finished. Then she made a motion with one finger against her brow and said, "You——" After that, however, she continued, "It seems to me quite enough that I do not remain away from here, even though I must expect that you are coming here at this time; but the place pleases me, and I see that you have brought me my sketch-book that I forgot here yesterday. I thank you for your vigilance. Won't you give it to me?" The last question was well founded, for he showed no disposition to do so, but remained motionless. It began to dawn upon him that he had imagined and worked out a monstrous piece of nonsense, and had also given expression to it; in order to compensate, as far as possible, he now stepped forward hastily, handed Gradiva the book, and at the same time sat down near her on the step, mechanically. Casting a glance at his hand, she said, "You seem to be a lover of roses."

At these words he suddenly became conscious 86of what had caused him to pluck and bring them and he responded, "Yes,—of course, not for myself, have I—you spoke yesterday—and last night, too, some one said it to me—people give them in spring."

She pondered briefly before she answered, "Ah, so—yes, I remember. To others, I meant, one does not give asphodel, but roses. That is polite of you; it seems your opinion of me is improved."

Her hand stretched out to receive the red flowers, and, handing them to her, he rejoined, "I believed at first that you could be here only during the noon hour, but it has become probable to me that you also, at some other time—that makes me very happy——"

"Why does it make you happy?"

Her face expressed lack of comprehension—only about her lips there passed a slight, hardly noticeable quiver. Confused, he offered, "It is beautiful to be alive; it has never seemed so much so to me before—I wished to ask you?" He searched in his breast pocket and added, as he drew out the object, "Has this brooch ever belonged to you?"

She leaned forward a little toward it, but shook her head. "No, I can't remember. Chronologically it would, of course, not be impossible, for it probably did not exist until this year. Did you find it in the sun perhaps? The beautiful green patina surely seems familiar to me, as if I had already seen it."

Involuntarily he repeated, "In the sun?—why in the sun?"

"'Sole' it is called here. It brings to light many things of that sort. Was the brooch said ⁸⁷to have belonged to a young girl who is said to have perished, I believe, in the vicinity of the Forum, with a companion?"

"Yes, who held his arm about her——"

"Ah, so——"

The two little words apparently lay upon Gradiva's tongue as a favourite interjection, and she stopped after it for a moment before she added, "Did you think that on that account I might have worn it? and would that have made you a little—how did you say it before?—unhappy?"

It was apparent that he felt extraordinarily relieved and it was audible in his answer, "I am very happy about it—for the idea that the brooch belonged to you made me—dizzy."

"You seem to have a tendency for that. Did you perhaps forget to eat breakfast this morning? That easily aggravates such attacks; I do not suffer from them, but I make provision, as it suits me best to be here at noon. If I can help you out of your unfortunate condition a little by sharing my lunch with you——"

She drew out of her pocket a piece of white bread wrapped in tissue paper, broke it, put half into his hand, and began to devour the other with apparent appetite. Thereby her exceptionally dainty and perfect teeth not only gleamed between her lips with pearly glitter, but in biting the crust caused also a crunching sound so that they gave the impression of being not unreal phantoms, but of actual, substantial reality. Besides, with her conjecture about the postponed breakfast, she had, to be sure, hit upon the right thing; mechanically he, too, ate, and felt from it ⁸⁸a decidedly favourable effect on the clearing of his thoughts. So, for a little while, the couple did not speak further, but devoted themselves silently to the same practical occupation until Gradiva said, "It seems to me as if we had already eaten our bread thus together once two thousand years ago. Can't you remember it?"

He could not, but it seemed strange to him now that she spoke of so infinitely remote a past, for the strengthening of his mind by the nourishment had brought with it a change in his brain. The idea that she had been going around here in Pompeii such a long time ago would no longer harmonize with sound reason; everything about her seemed of the present, as if it could be scarcely more than twenty years old. The form and colour of her face, the especially charming, brown, wavy hair, and the flawless teeth; also, the idea that the bright dress, marred by no shadow of a spot, had lain countless years in the pumice ashes contained something in the highest degree inconsistent. Norbert was seized by a feeling of doubt whether he were really sitting here awake or were not more probably dreaming in his study, where, in contemplation of the likeness of Gradiva, he had been overcome by sleep, and had dreamed that he had gone to Pompeii, had met her as a person still living, and was dreaming further that he was still sitting so at her side in the Casa di Meleagro. For that she was really still alive or had been living again could only have happened in a dream—the laws of nature raised an objection to it——

To be sure, it was strange that she had just ⁸⁹said that she had once shared her bread with him in that way two thousand years ago. Of that he knew nothing, and even in the dream could find nothing about it.

Her left hand lay with the slender fingers calmly on her knees. They bore the key to the solution of an inscrutable riddle——

Even in the dining-room of the Casa di Meleagro the boldness of the common house-fly was not deterred; on the yellow pillar opposite him he saw one running up and down in a worthless way in greedy quest; now it whizzed right past his nose.

He, however, had to make some answer to her question, if he did not remember the bread that he had formerly consumed with her, and he said suddenly, "Were the flies then as devilish as now, so that they tormented you to death?"

She glanced at him with utterly incomprehending astonishment and repeated, "The flies? Have you flies on your mind now?"

Then suddenly the black monster sat upon her hand, which did not reveal by the slightest quiver that she noticed it. Thereupon, however, there united in the young archæologist two powerful impulses to execute the same deed. His hand went up suddenly and clapped with no gentle stroke on the fly and the hand of his neighbour.

With this blow there came to him, for the first time, sense, consternation and also a joyous fear. He had delivered the stroke not through empty air, but on an undoubtedly real, living and warm, human hand which, for a moment apparently absolutely startled, remained motionless under his. Yet then she drew it away with a jerk, and the 90 mouth above it said, "You are surely apparently crazy, Norbert Hanold."

The name, which he had disclosed to no one in Pompeii, passed so easily, assuredly and clearly from her lips that its owner jumped up from the steps, even more terrified. At the same time there sounded in the colonnade footsteps of people who had come near unobserved; before his confused eyes appeared the faces of the congenial pair of lovers from the Casa del Fauno, and the young lady cried, with a tone of greatest surprise, "Zoë! You here, too? and also on your honeymoon? You have not written me a word about it, you know."

Norbert was again outside before Meleager's house in the Strada di Mercurio. How he had come there was not clear to him, it must have happened instinctively, and, caused by a lightning-like illumination in him, was the only thing that he could do not to present a thoroughly ridiculous figure to the young couple, even more to the girl greeted so pleasantly by them, who had just addressed him by his Christian and family names, and most of all to himself. For even if he grasped nothing, one fact was indisputable. Gradiva, with a warm, human hand, not unsubstantial, but possessing corporeal reality, had expressed an indubitable truth; his mind had, in the last two days, been in a condition of absolute madness; and not at all in a silly dream, but rather with the use of eyes and ears such as is given by nature to man for reasonable service. Like everything else, how such a thing had happened escaped his 91 understanding, and only darkly did he feel that there must have also been in the game a sixth sense which, obtaining the upper hand in some way, had transformed something perhaps precious to the opposite. In order to get at least a little more light on the matter by an attempt at meditation, a remote place in solitary silence was absolutely required; at first, however, he was impelled to withdraw as quickly as possible from the sphere of eyes, ears and other senses, which use their natural functions as suits their own purpose.

As for the owner of that warm hand, she had, at any rate, from her first expression, been surprised by the unforeseen and unexpected visit at noon in the Casa di Meleagro in a not entirely pleasant manner. Yet, of this, in the next instant, there was no trace to be seen in her bright countenance; she stood up quickly, stepped toward the young lady and said, extending her hand, "It certainly is pleasant, Gisa; chance sometimes has a clever idea too. So this is your husband of two weeks? I am glad to see him, and, from the appearance of both of you, I apparently need not change my congratulations for condolence. Couples to whom that would be applied are at this time usually sitting at lunch in Pompeii; you are probably staying near the 'ingresso'; I shall look you up there this afternoon. No, I have not written you anything; you won't be offended at me for that, for you see my hand, unlike yours, is not adorned by a ring. The atmosphere here has an extremely powerful effect on the imagination, which I can see in you; it is better, of course, than if it made one too matter-of-fact. The young 92 man who just went out is labouring also under a remarkable delusion; it seems to me that he believes a fly is buzzing in his head; well, everyone has, of course, some kind of bee in his bonnet. As is my duty, I have some knowledge of entomology and can, therefore, be of a little service in such cases. My father and I live in the 'Sole'; he, too, had a sudden and pleasing idea of bringing me here with him if I would be responsible for my own entertainment, and make no demands upon him. I said to myself that I should certainly dig up something interesting alone here. Of course I had not reckoned at all on the find which I made—I mean the good fortune of meeting you, Gisa; but I am talking away the time, as is usually the case with an old friend—— My father comes in out of the sun at two o'clock to eat at the 'Sole'; so I have to keep company there with his appetite and, therefore, I am sorry to say, must for the moment forego your society. You will, of course, be able to view the Casa di Meleagro without me; that I think likely, though I can't understand it, of course. Favorisca, signor! Arrivederci, Gisetta! That much Italian I have already learned, and one really does not need more. Whatever else is necessary one can invent—please, no, senza complimenti!"

This last entreaty of the speaker concerned a polite movement by which the young husband had seemed to wish to escort her. She had expressed herself most vividly, naturally and in a manner quite fitting to the circumstances of the unexpected meeting of a close friend, yet with extraordinary celerity, which testified to the urgency of the 93declaration that she could not at present remain longer. So not more than a few minutes had passed since the hasty exit of Norbert Hanold, when she stepped from the house of Meleager into the Strada di Mercurio. This lay, because of the hour, enlivened only here and there by a cringing lizard, and for a few moments the girl, hesitating, apparently gave herself over to a brief meditation. Then she quickly struck out in the shortest way to the gate of Hercules, at the intersection of the Vicolo di Mercurio and the Strada di Sallustio, crossed the stepping-stones with the gracefully buoyant Gradiva-walk, and thus arrived very quickly at the two ruins of the side wall near the Porta Ercolanese. Behind this there stretched at some length the Street of Tombs, yet not dazzlingly white, nor overhung with glittering sunbeams, as twenty-four hours ago, when the young archæologist had thus gazed down over it with searching eyes. To-day the sun seemed to be overcome by a feeling that she had done a little too much good in the morning; she held a grey veil drawn before her, the condensation of which was visibly being increased, and, as a result, the cypresses, which grew here and there in the Strada di Sepolcri, rose unusually sharp and black against the heavens. It was a picture different from that of yesterday; the brilliance which mysteriously glittered over everything was lacking; the street also assumed a certain gloomy distinctness, and had at present a dead aspect which honoured its name. This impression was not diminished by an isolated movement at its end, but was rather heightened by it; there, in the vicinity of the 94Villa of Diomede, a phantom seemed to be looking for its grave, and disappeared under one of the monuments.

It was not the shortest way from the house of Meleager to the "Albergo del Sole," rather the exactly opposite direction, but Zoë-Gradiva must have also decided that time was not yet importuning so violently to lunch, for after a quite brief stop at the Hercules Gate, she walked farther along the lava-blocks of the Street of Tombs, every time raising the sole of her lingering foot almost perpendicularly.

The Villa of Diomede—named thus, for people of the present, after a monument which a certain freed-man, Marcus Arrius Diomedes, formerly promoted to the directorship of this city-section, had erected near by for his lady, Arria, as well as for himself and his relatives—was a very extensive building and concealed within itself a part of the history of the destruction of Pompeii not invented by imagination. A confusion of extensive ruins formed the upper part; below lay an unusually large sunken garden surrounded by a well-preserved portico of pillars with scanty remnants of a fountain and a small temple in the middle; and farther along two stairways led down to a circular cellar-vault, lighted only dimly by gloomy twilight. The ashes of Vesuvius had penetrated into this also, and the skeletons of eighteen women and children had been found here; seeking protection they had fled, with some hastily gathered provisions, into the half-subterranean space, and the 95deceptive refuge had become the tomb of all. In another place the supposed, nameless master of the house lay, also stretched out choked on the ground; he had wished to escape through the locked garden-door, for he held the key to it in his fingers. Beside him cowered another skeleton, probably that of a servant, who was carrying a considerable number of gold and silver coins. The bodies of the unfortunates had been preserved by the hardened ashes; in the museum at Naples there is under glass, the exact impression of the neck, shoulders and beautiful bosom of a young girl clad in a fine, gauzy garment.

The Villa of Diomede had, at one time, at least, been the inevitable goal of every dutiful Pompeii visitor, but now, at noon, in its rather roomy solitude, certainly no curiosity lingered in it, and therefore it had seemed to Norbert Hanold the place of refuge best suited to his newest mental needs. These longed most insistently for grave-like loneliness, breathless silence, and quiescent peace; against the latter, however, an impelling restlessness in his system raised counter-claims, and he had been obliged to force an agreement between the two demands, such that the mind tried to claim its own and yet gave the feet liberty to follow their impulse. So he had been wandering around through the portico since his entrance; he succeeded thus in preserving his bodily equilibrium, and he busied himself with changing his mental state into the same normal condition; that, however, seemed more difficult in execution than in intention; of course it seemed to his judgment unquestionable that he had been utterly foolish [96]and irrational to believe that he had sat with a young Pompeiian girl, who had become more or less corporeally alive again, and this clear view of his madness formed incontestably an essential advance on the return to sound reason; but it was not yet restored entirely to normal condition, for, even if it had occurred to him that Gradiva was only a dead bas-relief, it was also equally beyond doubt that she was still alive. For that irrefutable proof was adduced; not he alone, but others also, saw her, knew that her name was Zoë and spoke with her, as with a being as much alive, in substance, as they. On the other hand, however, she knew his name too, and again, that could originate only from a supernatural power; this dual nature remained enigmatic even for the rays of understanding that were entering his mind. Yet to this incompatible duality there was joined a similar one in him, for he cherished the earnest desire to have been destroyed here in the Villa of Diomede two thousand years ago, in order that he might not run the risk of meeting Zoë-Gradiva again anywhere; at the same time, however, an extraordinary joyous feeling was stirring within him, because he was still alive and was therefore able to meet her again somewhere. To use a commonplace yet fitting simile, this was turning in his head like a mill-wheel, and through the long portico he ran around likewise without stopping, which did not aid him in the explanation of the contradictions. On the contrary, he was moved by an indefinite feeling that everything was growing darker and darker about and within him.

Then he suddenly recoiled, as he turned one of [97]the four corners of the colonnade. A half-dozen paces away from him there sat, rather high up on a fragmentary wall-ruin, one of the young girls who had found death here in the ashes.

No, that was nonsense, which his reason rejected. His eyes, too, and a nameless something else recognized that fact. It was Gradiva; she was sitting on a stone ruin as she had formerly sat on the step, only, as the former was considerably higher, her slender feet, which hung down free in the sand-colour shoes, were visible up to her dainty ankles.

With an instinctive movement, Norbert was at first about to run out between the pillars through the garden; what, for a half-hour, he had feared most of anything in the world had suddenly appeared, viewed him with bright eyes and with lips which, he felt, were about to burst into mocking laughter; yet they didn't, but the familiar voice rang out calmly from them, "You'll get wet outside."

Now, for the first time, he saw that it was raining; for that reason it had become so dark. That unquestionably was an advantage to all the plants about and in Pompeii, but that a human being in the place would be benefited by it was ridiculous, and for the moment Norbert Hanold feared, far more than danger of death, appearing ridiculous. Therefore he involuntarily gave up the attempt to get away, stood there, helpless, and looked at the two feet, which now, as if somewhat impatient, were swinging back and forth; and as this view did not have so clearing an effect upon his thoughts that he could find expression for them, the owner [98]of the dainty feet again took up the conversation. "We were interrupted before; you were just going to tell me something about flies—I imagined that you were making scientific investigations here—or about a fly in your head. Did you succeed in catching and destroying the one on my hand?"

This last she said with a smiling expression about her lips, which, however, was so faint and charming that it was not at all terrifying. On the contrary, it now lent to the questioned man power of speech, but with this limitation, that the young archæologist suddenly did not know how to address her. In order to escape this dilemma, he found it best to avoid that and replied, "I was—as they say—somewhat confused mentally and ask pardon that I—the hand—in that way—how I could be so stupid, I can't understand—but I can't understand either how its owner could use my name in upbraiding me for my—my madness."

Gradiva's feet stopped moving and she rejoined, still addressing him familiarly, "Your power of understanding has not yet progressed that far, Norbert Hanold. Of course, I cannot be surprised, for you have long ago accustomed me to it. To make that discovery again I should not have needed to come to Pompeii, and you could have confirmed it for me a good hundred miles nearer."

"A hundred miles nearer"—he repeated, perplexed and half stuttering—"where is that?"

"Diagonally across from your house, in the corner house; in my window, in a cage, is a canary."

Like a memory from far away this last word moved the hearer, who repeated, "A canary"—and he added, stuttering more—"He—he sings?"

99"They usually do, especially in spring when the sun begins to seem warm again. In that house lives my father, Richard Bertgang, professor of zoology."

Norbert Hanold's eyes opened to a width never before attained by them, and then he said, "Bertgang—then are you—are you—Miss Zoë Bertgang? But she looked quite different——"

The two dangling feet began again to swing a little, and Miss Zoë Bertgang said in reply, "If you find that form of address more suitable between us, I can use it too, you know, but the other came to me more naturally. I don't know whether I looked different when we used to run about before with each other as friends every day, and occasionally beat and cuffed each other, for a change, but if, in recent years, you had favoured me with even one glance, you might perhaps have seen that I have looked like this for a long time.—No, now, as they say, it's pouring pitchforks; you won't have a dry stitch."

Not only had the feet of the speaker indicated a return of impatience, or whatever it might be, but also in the tones of her voice there appeared a little didactic, ill-humoured curtness, and Norbert had thereby been overwhelmed by a feeling that he was running the risk of slipping into the rôle of a big school-boy scolded and slapped in the face. That caused him to again seek mechanically for an exit between the pillars, and to the movement which showed this impulse Miss Zoë's last utterance, indifferently added, had reference; and, of course, in an undeniably striking way, because for what was now occurring outside of the shelter, 100"pouring" was really a mild term. A tropical cloudburst such as only seldom took pity on the summer thirst of the meadows of the Campagna, was shooting vertically and rushing as if the Tyrrhenian Sea were pouring from heaven upon the Villa of Diomede, and yet it continued like a firm wall composed of billions of drops gleaming like pearls and large as nuts. That, indeed, made escape out into the open air impossible, and forced Norbert Hanold to remain in the school-room of the portico while the young school-mistress with the delicate, clever face made use of the hindrance for further extension of her pedagogical discussion by continuing, after a brief pause:—

"Then up to the time when people call us 'Backfisch,' for some unknown reason, I had really acquired a remarkable attachment for you and thought that I could never find a more pleasing friend in the world. Mother, sister, or brother I had not, you know; to my father a slow-worm in alcohol was far more interesting than I, and people (I count girls such) must surely have something with which they can occupy their thoughts and the like. Then you were that something, but when archæology overcame you, I made the discovery that you—excuse the familiarity, but your new formality sounds absurd to me—I was saying that I imagined that you had become an intolerable person, who had no longer, at least for me, an eye in his head, a tongue in his mouth, nor any of the memories that I retained of our childhood friendship. So I probably looked different from what I did formerly, for when, occasionally, I met you at a party, even last winter, you did not look at me 101and I did not hear your voice; in this, of course, there was nothing which marked me out especially, for you treated all the others in the same way. To you I was but air, and you, with your shock of light hair, which I had formerly pulled so often, were as boresome, dry and tongue-tied as a stuffed cockatoo and at the same time as grandiose as an—archæopteryx; I believe the excavated, antediluvian bird-monster is so called; but that your head harboured an imagination so magnificent as here in Pompeii to consider me something excavated and restored to life—I had not surmised that of you, and when you suddenly stood before me unexpectedly, it cost me some effort at first to understand what kind of incredible fancy your imagination had invented. Then I was amused, and, in spite of its madness, it was not entirely displeasing to me. For, as I said, I had not expected it of you."

With that, her expression and tone somewhat mollified at the end, Miss Zoë Bertgang finished her unreserved, detailed and instructive lecture, and it was indeed notable how exactly she then resembled the figure of Gradiva on the bas-relief, not only in her features, her form, her eyes, expressive of wisdom, and her charmingly wavy hair, but also in her graceful manner of walking which he had often seen; her drapery, too, dress and scarf of a cream-coloured, fine cashmere material which fell in soft, voluminous folds, completed the extraordinary resemblance of her whole appearance. There might have been much foolishness in the belief that a young Pompeiian girl, destroyed two thousand years ago by Vesuvius, 102could sometimes walk around alive again, speak, draw and eat bread, but even if the belief brought happiness, it assumed everywhere, in the bargain, a considerable amount of incomprehensibility; and in consideration of all the circumstances, there was incontestably present, in the judgment of Norbert Hanold, some mitigating ground for his madness in for two days considering Gradiva a resurrection.

Although he stood there dry under the portico roof, there was established, not quite ineptly, a comparison between him and a wet poodle, who has had a bucketful of water thrown on his head; but the cold shower-bath had really done him good. Without knowing exactly why, he felt that he was breathing much more easily. In that, of course, the change of tone at the end of the sermon—for the speaker sat as if in a pulpit-chair—might have helped especially; at least thereat a transfigured light appeared in his eyes, such as awakened hope for salvation through faith produces in the eyes of an ardently affected church-attendant; and as the rebuke was now over, and there seemed no necessity for fearing a further continuation, he succeeded in saying, "Yes, now I recognize—no, you have not changed at all—it is you, Zoë—my good, happy, clever comrade—it is most strange——"

"That a person must die to become alive again; but for archæologists that is of course necessary."

"No, I mean your name——"

"Why is it strange?"

The young archæologist showed himself familiar with not only the classical languages, but also with the etymology of German, and continued, 103"Because Bertgang has the same meaning as Gradiva and signifies 'the one splendid in walking.'"

Miss Zoë Bertgang's two sandal-like shoes were, for the moment, because of their movement, reminiscent of an impatiently see-sawing wagtail waiting for something; yet the possessor of the feet which walked so magnificently seemed not at present to be paying any attention to philological explanations; by her countenance she gave the impression of being occupied with some hasty plan, but was restrained from it by an exclamation of Norbert Hanold's which audibly emanated from deepest conviction, "What luck, though, that you are not Gradiva, but are like the congenial young lady!"

That caused an expression as of interested surprise to pass over her face, and she asked, "Who is that? Whom do you mean?"

"The one who spoke to you in Meleager's house."

"Do you know her?"

"Yes, I had already seen her. She was the first person who seemed especially congenial to me."

"So? Where did you see her?"

"This morning, in the House of the Faun. There the couple were doing something very strange."

"What were they doing?"

"They did not see me and they kissed each other."

"That was really very reasonable, you know. Why else are they in Pompeii on their wedding trip?"

At one blow with the last word the former 104picture changed before Norbert Hanold's eyes, for the old wall-ruin lay there empty, because the girl, who had chosen it as a seat, teacher's chair and pulpit, had come down, or really flown, and with the same supple buoyancy as that of a wagtail swinging through the air, so that she already stood again on Gradiva-feet, before his glance had consciously caught up with her descent; and continuing her speech directly, she said, "Well, the rain has stopped; too severe rulers do not reign long. That is reasonable, too, you know, and thus everything has again become reasonable. I, not least of all, and you can look up Gisa Hartleben, or whatever new name she has, to be of scientific assistance to her about the purpose of her stay in Pompeii. I must now go to the 'Albergo del Sole,' for my father is probably waiting for me already at lunch. Perhaps we shall meet again sometime at a party in Germany or on the moon. Addio!"

Zoë Bertgang said this in the absolutely polite, but also equally indifferent tone of a most well-bred young lady, and, as was her custom, placing her left foot forward, raised the sole of the right almost perpendicularly to pass out. As she lifted her dress slightly with her left hand, because of the thoroughly wet ground outside, the resemblance to Gradiva was perfect and the man, standing hardly more than two arm-lengths away, noticed for the first time a quite insignificant deviation in the living picture from the stone one. The latter lacked something possessed by the former, which appeared at the moment quite clear, a little dimple in her cheek, which produced a slight, indefinable effect. It puckered and wrinkled a 105little and could therefore express annoyance or a suppressed impulse to laugh, possibly both together. Norbert Hanold looked at it and although from the evidence just presented to him he had completely regained his reason, his eyes had to again submit to an optical illusion. For, in a tone triumphing peculiarly over his discovery, he cried out, "There is the fly again!"

It sounded so strange that from the incomprehending listener, who could not see herself, escaped the question, "The fly—where?"

"There on your cheek!" and immediately the man, as he answered, suddenly twined an arm about her neck and snapped, this time with his lips, at the insect so deeply abhorrent to him, which vision juggled before his eyes deceptively in the little dimple. Apparently, however, without success, for right afterwards he cried again, "No, now it's on your lips!" and thereupon, quick as a flash, he directed thither his attempt to capture, now remaining so long that no doubt could survive that he succeeded in completely accomplishing his purpose, and strange to relate the living Gradiva did not hinder him at all, and when her mouth, after about a minute, was forced to struggle for breath, restored to powers of speech, she did not say, "You are really crazy, Norbert Hanold," but rather allowed a most charming smile to play more visibly than before about her red lips; she had been convinced more than ever of the complete recovery of his reason.

The Villa of Diomede had two thousand years ago seen and heard horrible things in an evil hour, yet at the present it heard and saw, for about an 106hour, only things not at all suited to inspire horror. Then, however, a sensible idea became uppermost in Miss Zoë Bertgang's mind and as a result, she said, against her wishes, "Now, I must *really* go, or my poor father will starve. It seems to me you can to-day forego Gisa Hartleben's company at noon, for you have nothing more to learn from her and ought to be content with us in the 'Sun Hotel.'"

From this it was to be concluded that daring that hour something must have been discussed, for it indicated a helpful desire to instruct, which the young lady vented on Norbert. Yet, from the reminding words, he did not gather this, but something which, for the first time, he was becoming terribly conscious of; this was apparent in the repetition, "Your father—what will he——?"

Miss Zoë, however, interrupted, without any sign of awakened anxiety, "Probably he will do nothing; I am not an indispensable piece in his zoological collection; if I were, my heart would probably not have clung to you so unwisely. Besides, from my early years, I have been sure that a woman is of use in the world only when she relieves a man of the trouble of deciding household matters; I generally do this for my father, and therefore you can also be rather at ease about your future. Should he, however, by chance, in this case, have an opinion different from mine, we will make it as simple as possible. You go over to Capri for a couple of days; there, with a grass snare—you can practise making them on my little finger—catch a lizard *Faraglionensis*. Let it go here again, and catch it before his eyes. [107]Then give him free choice between it and me, and you will have me so surely that I am sorry for you. Toward his colleague, Eimer, however, I feel to-day that I have formerly been ungrateful, for without his genial invention of lizard-catching I should probably not have come into Meleager's house, and that would have been a shame, not only for you, but for me too."

This last view she expressed outside of the Villa of Diomede and, alas, there was no person present on earth who could make any statements about the voice and manner of talking of Gradiva. Yet even if they had resembled those of Zoë Bertgang, as everything else about her did, they must have possessed a quite unusually beautiful and roguish charm.

By this, at least, Norbert Hanold was so strongly overwhelmed that, exalted to poetic flights, he cried out, "Zoë, you dear life and lovely present—we shall take our wedding-trip to Italy and Pompeii."

That was a decided proof of how different circumstances can also produce a transformation in a human being and at the same time unite with it a weakening of the memory. For it did not occur to him at all that he would thereby expose himself and his companion on the journey to the danger of receiving, from misanthropic, ill-humoured railway companions, the names Augustus and Gretchen, but at the moment he was thinking so little about it that they walked along hand in hand through the old Street of Tombs in Pompeii. Of course this, too, did not stamp itself into their minds at present as such, for a cloudless sky shone and laughed again above it; the sun stretched [108]out a golden carpet on the old lava-blocks; Vesuvius spread its misty pine-cone; and the whole excavated city seemed overwhelmed, not with pumice and ashes, but with pearls and diamonds, by the beneficent rain-storm.

The brilliance in the eyes of the young daughter of the zoologist rivalled these, but to the announced desire about the destination of their journey by her childhood friend who had, in a way, also been excavated from the ashes, her wise lips responded: "I think we won't worry about that to-day; that is a thing which may better be left by both of us to more and maturer consideration and future promptings. I, at least, do not yet feel quite alive enough now for such geographical decisions."

That showed that the speaker possessed great modesty about the quality of her insight into things about which she had never thought until to-day. They had arrived again at the Hercules Gate, where, at the beginning of the Strada Consolare, old stepping-stones crossed the street. Norbert Hanold stopped before them and said with a peculiar tone, "Please go ahead here." A merry, comprehending, laughing expression lurked around his companion's mouth, and, raising her dress slightly with her left hand, Gradiva *rediviva*Zoë Bertgang, viewed by him with dreamily observing eyes, crossed with her calmly buoyant walk, through the sunlight, over the stepping-stones, to the other side of the street.

[109]

PART II
DELUSION AND DREAM
IN
WILHELM JENSEN'S *GRADIVA*
BY
DR. SIGMUND FREUD

[111]

DELUSION AND DREAM
I

In a circle of men who take it for granted that the basic riddle of the dream has been solved by the efforts of the present writer,[1] curiosity was aroused one day concerning those dreams which have never been dreamed, those created by authors, and attributed to fictitious characters in their productions. The proposal to submit this kind of dream to investigation might appear idle and strange; but from one view-point it could be considered justifiable. It is, to be sure, not at all generally believed that the dreamer dreams something senseful and significant. Science and the majority of educated people smile when one offers them the task of interpreting dreams. Only people still clinging to superstition, who give continuity, thereby, to the convictions of the ancients, will not refrain from interpreting dreams, and the writer of *Traumdeutung* has dared, against the protests of orthodox science, to take sides with the ancients and superstitious. He is, of course, far from accepting in dreams a prevision of the future, for the disclosure of which man has, from time immemorial, 112striven vainly. He could not, however, completely reject the connections of dreams with the future, for, after completing some arduous analysis, the dreams seemed to him to represent *the fulfilment of a wish* of the dreamer; and who could dispute that wishes are preponderantly concerned with the future?

I have just said that the dream is a fulfilled wish. Whoever is not afraid to toil through a difficult book, whoever does not demand that a complicated problem be insincerely and untruthfully presented to him as easy and simple, to save his own effort, may seek in the above-mentioned *Traumdeutung* ample proof of this statement, and may, until then, cast aside the objection that will surely be expressed against the equivalence of dreams and wish-fulfilment.

We have, however, anticipated. The question is not now one of establishing whether the meaning of a dream is, in every case, to be interpreted as the fulfilment of a wish, or, just as frequently, as an anxious expectation, an intention or deliberation, etc. The first question is, rather, whether the dream has any meaning at all, whether one should grant it the value of a psychic process. Science answers, *No*; it explains the dream as a purely physiological process, behind which one need not seek meaning, significance nor intention. Physical excitations play, during sleep, on the psychic instrument and bring into consciousness sometimes some, sometimes other ideas devoid of psychic coherence. Dreams are comparable only to convulsions, not to expressive movements.

In this dispute over the estimation of dreams, writers seem to stand on the same side with the 113ancients, superstitious people and the author of *Traumdeutung*. For, when they cause the people created by their imagination to dream, they follow the common experience that people's thoughts and feelings continue into sleep, and they seek only to depict the psychic states of their heroes through the dreams of the latter. Story-tellers are valuable allies, and their testimony is to be rated high, for they usually know many things between heaven and earth that our academic wisdom does not even dream of. In psychic knowledge, indeed, they are far ahead of us ordinary people, because they draw from sources that we have not yet made accessible for science. Would that this partizanship of literary workers for the senseful nature of dreams were only more unequivocal! Sharper criticism might object that writers take sides neither for nor against the psychic significance of an isolated dream; they are satisfied to show how the sleeping psyche stirs under the stimuli which have remained active in it as off-shoots of waking life.

Our interest for the way in which story-tellers make use of dreams is not, however, made less intense by this disillusionment. Even if the investigation should teach nothing of the nature of dreams, it may perhaps afford us, from this angle, a little insight into the nature of creative literary production. Actual dreams are considered to be unrestrained and irregular formations, and now come the free copies of such dreams; but there is much less freedom and arbitrariness in psychic life than we are inclined to believe, perhaps none at all. What we, laity, call chance resolves itself, to an acknowledged degree, into laws; also, what we call 114arbitrariness in psychic life rests on laws only now dimly surmised. Let us see!

There are two possible methods for this investigation; one is engrossment with a special case, with the dream-creations of one writer in one of his works; the other consists in bringing together and comparing all the examples of the use of dreams which are found in the works of different story-tellers. The second way seems to be by far the more effective, perhaps the only justifiable one, for it frees us immediately from the dangers connected with the conception of "the writer" as an artistic unity. This unity falls to pieces in investigations of widely different writers, among whom we are wont to honour some, individually, as the most profound connoisseurs of psychic life. Yet these pages will be filled by an investigation of the former kind. It so happened, in the group of men who started the idea, that some one remembered that the bit of fiction which he had most recently enjoyed contained several dreams which looked at him with familiar expression and invited him to try on them the method of *Traumdeutung*. He admitted that the material and setting of the little tale had been partly responsible for the origin of his pleasure, for the story was unfolded in Pompeii, and concerned a young archæologist who had given up interest in life, for that in the remains of the classic past, and now, by a remarkable but absolutely correct détour, was brought back to life. During the perusal of this really poetic material, the reader experienced all sorts of feelings of familiarity and concurrence. The tale was Wilhelm Jensen's *Gradiva*, a little 115romance designated by its author himself "A Pompeian Fancy."

In order that my further references may be to familiar material, I must now ask my readers to lay aside this pamphlet, and replace it for some time with *Gradiva*, which first appeared in the book world in 1903. To those who have already read *Gradiva*, I will recall the content of the story in a short epitome, and hope that their memory will of itself restore all the charm of which the story is thereby stripped.

A young archæologist, Norbert Hanold, has discovered at Rome, in a collection of antiques, a bas-relief which attracts him so exceptionally that he is delighted to be able to get an excellent plaster-cast of it which he can hang up in his study in a German university-city and study with interest. The relief represents a mature young girl walking. She has gathered up her voluminous gown slightly, so that her sandalled feet become visible. One foot rests wholly on the ground; the other is raised to follow and touches the ground only with the tips of the toes while sole and heel rise almost perpendicularly. The unusual and especially charming walk represented had probably aroused the artist's attention, and now, after so many centuries, captivates the eye of our archæological observer.

This interest of the hero in the described bas-relief is the basic psychological fact of our story. It is not immediately explicable. "Doctor Norbert Hanold, docent of archæology, really found in the relief nothing noteworthy for his science." (*Gradiva*, p. 14.) "He could not explain what quality in it had aroused his attention; he knew 116only that he had been attracted by something and this effect of the first view had remained unchanged since then," but his imagination does not cease to be occupied with the relief. He finds in it a "sense of present time," as if the artist had fixed the picture on the street "from life." He confers upon the girl represented walking a name, Gradiva, "the girl splendid in walking," spins a yarn that she is the daughter of a distinguished family, perhaps of a "patrician ædile, whose office was connected with the worship of Ceres," and is on the way to the temple of the goddess. Then it is repulsive to him to place her in the mob of a metropolis; rather he convinces himself that she is to be transported to Pompeii, and is walking there somewhere on the peculiar stepping-stones which have been excavated; these made a dry crossing possible in rainy weather, and yet also afforded passage for chariot-wheels. The cut of her features seems to him Greek, her Hellenic ancestry unquestionable. All of his science of antiquity gradually puts itself at the service of this or other fancies connected with the relief.

Then, however, there obtrudes itself upon him a would-be scientific problem which demands solution. Now it is a matter of his passing a critical judgment "whether the artist had reproduced Gradiva's manner of walking from life." He cannot produce it in himself; in the search for the "real existence" of this gait, he arrives only at "observation from life for the purpose of enlightenment on the matter" (*G*. p. 18). This forces him, to be sure, to a mode of action utterly foreign to him. "Women had formerly been for 117him only a conception in marble or bronze, and he had never given his feminine contemporaries the least consideration." Society life has always seemed to him an unavoidable torture; young ladies whom he meets, in such connections, he fails to see and hear, to such a degree that, on the next encounter, he passes without greeting, which, of course, serves to place him in an unfavourable light with them. Now, however, the scientific task which he has imposed upon himself forces him in dry weather, but especially in wet weather, to observe diligently the feet of ladies and girls on the street, an activity which yields him many a displeased and many an encouraging glance from those observed. "Yet one was as incomprehensible to him as the other." (*G*. p. 19.) As a result of these careful studies, he finds that Gradiva's gait cannot be proved to exist really, a fact which fills him with regret and annoyance.

Soon afterwards he has a terribly frightful dream, which transports him to old Pompeii on the day of the eruption of Vesuvius, and makes him an eye-witness of the destruction of the city. "As he stood thus at the edge of the Forum near the Jupiter temple, he suddenly saw Gradiva a short distance in front of him. Until then no thought of her presence there had moved him, but now suddenly it seemed natural to him, as she was, of course, a Pompeiian girl, that she was living in her native city and, *without his having any suspicion of it, was his contemporary.*" (*G.* p. 20.) Fear about her impending fate draws from him a cry of warning, in answer to which the unperturbed apparition turns her face toward him. [118]Unconcerned, she continues her way to the portico of the temple, sits down there on a step and slowly rests her head upon it, while her face keeps growing paler, as if it were turning to white marble. As he hastens after her, he finds her, with calm countenance, stretched out, as if sleeping, on the broad step; soon the rain of ashes buries her form.

When he awakes, he thinks he is still hearing the confused cries of the Pompeiians, who are seeking safety, and the dully resounding boom of the turbulent sea; but even after his returning senses have recognized these noises as the waking expressions of life in the noisy metropolis, he retains for some time the belief in the reality of what he has dreamed; when he has finally rid himself of the idea that he was really present, nearly two thousand years ago, at the destruction of Pompeii, there yet remains to him, as a firm conviction, the idea that Gradiva lived in Pompeii and was buried there in the year 79. His fancies about Gradiva, due to the after-effects of this dream, continue so that he now, for the first time, begins to mourn her as lost.

While he leans from his window, prepossessed with these ideas, a canary, warbling his song in a cage at an open window of the house opposite, attracts his attention. Suddenly something like a thrill passes through the man not yet completely awakened from his dream. He believes that he sees, in the street, a figure like that of his Gradiva, and even recognizes the gait characteristic of her; without deliberation he hastens to the street to overtake her, and the laughter and jeers of the people, at his unconventional morning attire, first [119]drive him quickly back home. In his room, it is again the singing canary in the cage who occupies him and stimulates him to a comparison with himself. He, too, is sitting in a cage, he finds, yet it is easier for him to leave his cage. As if from added after-effect of the dream, perhaps also under the influence of the mild spring air, he decides to take a spring trip to Italy, for which a scientific motive is soon found, even if "the impulse for travel had originated in a nameless feeling" (*G.* p. 28).

We will stop a moment at this most loosely motivated journey and take a closer look at the personality, as well as the activities of our hero. He seems to us still incomprehensible and foolish; we have no idea of how his special folly is to acquire enough human appeal to compel our interest. It is the privilege of the author of *Gradiva* to leave us in such a quandary; with his beauty of diction and his judicious selection of incident, he presently rewards our confidence and the undeserved sympathy which we still grant to his hero. Of the latter we learn that he is already destined by family tradition to be an antiquarian, has later, in isolation and independence, submerged himself completely in his science, and has withdrawn entirely from life and its pleasures. Marble and bronze are, for his feelings, the only things really alive and expressing the purpose and value of human life. Yet, perhaps with kind intent, Nature has put into his blood a thoroughly unscientific sort of corrective, a most lively imagination, which can impress itself not only on his dreams, but also on his waking life. By such separation of imagination and intellectual capacity, he is destined to be [120]a poet or a neurotic, and he belongs to that race of beings whose realm is not of this world. So it happens that his interest is fixed upon a bas-relief which represents a girl walking in an unusual manner, that he spins a web of fancies about it, invents a name and an ancestry for it, and transports the person created by him into Pompeii, which was buried more than eighteen hundred years ago. Finally, after a remarkable anxiety-dream he intensifies the fancy of the existence and destruction of the girl named Gradiva into a delusion which comes to influence his acts. These performances of imagination would appear to us strange and inscrutable, if we should encounter them in a really living person. As our hero, Norbert Hanold, is a creature of an author, we should like to ask the latter timidly if his fancy has been determined by any power other than his own arbitrariness.

We left our hero just as he is apparently being moved by the song of a canary to take a trip to Italy, the motive for which is apparently not clear to him. We learn, further, that neither destination nor purpose are firmly established in his mind. An inner restlessness and dissatisfaction drive him from Rome to Naples and farther on from there; he encounters the swarm of honeymoon travellers, and, forced to notice the tender "Augustuses" and "Gretchens," is utterly unable to understand the acts and impulses of the couples. He arrives at the conclusion that, of all the follies of humanity, "marriage, at any rate, took the prize as the greatest and most incomprehensible one, and the senseless wedding trips to Italy somehow capped the climax of this buffoonery." 121(G. p. 30.) At Rome, disturbed in his sleep by the proximity of a loving couple, he flees, forthwith, to Naples, only to find there another "Augustus" and "Gretchen." As he believes that he understands from their conversation that the majority of those bird-couples does not intend to nest in the rubbish of Pompeii, but to take flight to Capri, he decides to do what they do not do, and finds himself in Pompeii, "contrary to expectations and intentions," a few days after the beginning of his journey—without, however, finding there the peace which he seeks.

The rôle which, until then, has been played by the honeymoon couples, who made him uneasy and vexed his senses, is now assumed by house-flies, in which he is inclined to see the incarnation of absolute evil and worthlessness. The two tormentors blend into one; many fly-couples remind him of honeymoon travellers, address each other probably, in their language, also as "My only Augustus" and "My sweet Gretchen."

Finally he cannot help admitting "that his dissatisfaction was certainly caused not by his surroundings alone, but to a degree found its origin in him." (G. p. 40.) He feels that he is out of sorts because he lacks something without being able to explain what.

The next morning he goes through the "ingresso" to Pompeii and, after taking leave of the guide, roams aimlessly through the city, notably, however, without remembering that he has been present in a dream some time before at the destruction of Pompeii. Therefore in the "hot, holy" hour of noon, which the ancients, you know, 122considered the ghost-hour, when the other visitors have taken flight and the heap of ruins, desolate and steeped in sunlight, lies before him, there stirs in him the ability to transport himself back into the buried life, but not with the aid of science. "What it taught was a lifeless, archæological view and what came from its mouth was a dead, philological language. These helped in no way to a comprehension with soul, mind and heart, as the saying is, but he, who possessed a desire for that, had to stand alone here, the only living person in the hot noonday silence, among the remains of the past, in order not to see with physical eyes nor hear with corporeal ears. Then—the dead awoke, and Pompeii began to live again." (G. p. 48.) While thus, by means of his imagination, he endows the past with life, he suddenly sees, indubitably, the Gradiva of his bas-relief step out of a house and buoyantly cross the lava stepping-stones, just as he had seen her in the dream that night when she had lain down to sleep on the steps of the Apollo temple. "With this memory he became conscious, for the first time, of something else; he had, without himself knowing the motive in his heart, come to Italy on that account, and had, without stop, continued from Rome and Naples to Pompeii to see if he could here find trace of her—and that in a literal sense—for, with her unusual gait, she must have left behind in the ashes a foot-print different from all the others." (G. p. 50.)

The suspense, in which the author of *Gradiva* has kept us up to this point, mounts here, for a moment, to painful confusion. Not only because 123our hero has apparently lost his equilibrium, but also because, confronted with the appearance of Gradiva, who was formerly a plaster-cast and then a creation of imagination, we are lost. Is it a hallucination of our deluded hero, a "real" ghost, or a corporeal person? Not that we need to believe in ghosts to draw up this list. Jensen, who named his tale a "Fancy," has, of course, found no occasion, as yet, to explain to us whether he wishes to leave us in our world, decried as dull and ruled by the laws of science, or to conduct us into another fantastic one, in which reality is ascribed to ghosts and spirits. As *Hamlet* and *Macbeth* show, we are ready to follow him into such a place without hesitation. The delusion of the imaginative archæologist would need, in that case, to be measured by another standard. Yes, when we consider how improbable must be the real existence of a person who faithfully reproduces in her appearance that antique bas-relief, our list shrinks to an alternative: hallucination or ghost of the noon hour. A slight touch in the description eliminates the former possibility. A large lizard lies stretched out, motionless, in the sunlight; it flees, however, before the approaching foot of Gradiva and wriggles away over the lava pavement. So, no hallucination; something outside of the mind of our dreamer. But ought the reality of a *rediviva* to be able to disturb a lizard?

Before the house of Meleager Gradiva disappears. We are not surprised that Norbert Hanold persists in his delusion that Pompeii has begun to live again about him in the noon hour of spirits, and that Gradiva has also returned to life and gone into |24the house where she lived before the fateful August day of the year 79. There dart through his mind keen conjectures about the personality of the owner, after whom the house may have been named, and about Gradiva's relation to the latter; these show that his science has now given itself over completely to the service of his imagination. After entering this house, he again suddenly discovers the apparition, sitting on low steps between two yellow pillars. "Spread out on her knees lay something white, which he was unable to distinguish clearly; it seemed to be a papyrus sheet" (*G.* p. 55). Taking for granted his most recent suppositions about her ancestry, he speaks to her in Greek, awaiting timorously the determination of whether the power of speech may, perhaps, be granted to her in her phantom existence. As she does not answer, he changes the greeting to Latin. Then, from smiling lips, come the words, "If you wish to speak with me, you must do so in German."

What embarrassment for us, the readers! Thus the author of *Gradiva* has made sport of us and decoyed us, as if by means of the refulgence of Pompeiian sunshine, into a little delusion so that we may be milder in our judgment of the poor man, whom the real noonday sun actually burns; but we know now, after recovering from brief confusion, that Gradiva is a living German girl, a fact which we wish to reject as utterly improbable. Reflecting calmly, we now await a discovery of what connection exists between the girl and the stone representation of her, and of how our young archæologist acquired the fancies which hint at her real personality.

|25Our hero is not freed so quickly as we from the delusion, for, "Even if the belief brought happiness," says our author, "it assumed everywhere, in the bargain, a considerable amount of incomprehensibility." (*G.* p. 102.) Besides, this delusion probably has subjective roots of which we know nothing, which do not exist for us. He doubtless needs trenchant treatment to bring him back to reality. For the present he can do nothing but adapt the delusion to the wonderful discovery which he has just made. Gradiva, who had perished at the destruction of Pompeii, can be nothing but a ghost of the noon hour, who returns to life for the noon hour of spirits; but why, after the answer given in German, does the exclamation escape him: "I knew that your voice sounded like that"? Not only we, but the girl, too, must ask, and Hanold must admit that he has never heard her voice before, but expected to hear it in the dream, when he called to her, as she lay down to sleep on the steps of the temple. He begs her to repeat that action, but she then rises, directs a strange glance at him, and, after a few steps, disappears between the pillars of the court. A beautiful butterfly had, shortly before that, fluttered about her a few times; in his interpretation it had been a messenger from Hades, who was to admonish the departed one to return, as the noon hour of spirits had passed. The call, "Are you coming here again to-morrow in the noon hour?" Hanold can send after the disappearing girl. To us, however, who venture a more sober interpretation, it will seem that the young lady found something improper in the request which |26Hanold had made of her, and therefore, insulted, left him, as she could yet know nothing of his dream. May not her delicacy of feeling have realized the erotic nature of the request, which was prompted, for Hanold, only by the connection with his dream?

After the disappearance of Gradiva, our hero examines all the guests at the "Hotel Diomed" table and soon also those of "Hotel Suisse," and can then assure himself that in neither of the only two lodgings known to him in Pompeii is a person to be found who possesses the most remote resemblance to Gradiva. Of course he had rejected, as unreasonable, the supposition that he might really meet Gradiva in one of the two hostelries. The wine pressed on the hot soil of Vesuvius then helps to increase the day's dizziness.

The only certainty about the next day is that Norbert must again be in Meleager's house at noon; and, awaiting the hour, he enters Pompeii over the old city-wall, a way which is against the rules. An asphodel cluster of white bell-flowers seems, as flower of the lower world, significant enough for him to pluck and carry away. All his knowledge of antiquity appears to him, however, while he is waiting, as the most purposeless and indifferent matter in the world, for another interest has acquired control of him, the problem, "what is the nature of the physical manifestation of a being like Gradiva, dead and alive at the same time, although the latter was true only in the noon hour of spirits?" (G. p. 64.) He is also worried lest to-day he may not meet the lady sought, because perhaps she may not be allowed [127] to return for a long time, and when he again sees her between the pillars, he considers her appearance an illusion, which draws from him the grieved exclamation, "Oh, that you were still alive!" This time, however, he has evidently been too critical, for the apparition possesses a voice which asks him whether he wishes to bring her the white flower, and draws the man, who has again lost his composure, into a long conversation. Our author informs us, readers, to whom Gradiva has already become interesting as a living personality, that the ill-humoured and repellent glance of the day before has given way to an expression of searching inquisitiveness or curiosity. She really sounds him, demands, in explanation of his remark of the preceding day, when he had stood near her as she lay down to sleep, in this way learns of the dream in which she perished with her native city, then of the bas-relief, and of the position of the foot, which attracted the young archæologist. Now she shows herself ready to demonstrate her manner of walking, whereby the substitution of light, sand-coloured, fine leather shoes for the sandals, which she explains as adaptation to the present, is established as the only deviation from the original relief of Gradiva. Apparently she is entering into his delusion, whose whole range she elicits from him, without once opposing him. Only once she seems to have been wrested from her rôle by a peculiar feeling when, his mind on the bas-relief, he asserts that he has recognized her at first glance. As, at this stage of the conversation, she, as yet, knows nothing of the relief, she must be on the point of misunderstanding Hanold's words, but she has [128] immediately recovered herself again, and only to us will many of her speeches appear to have a double meaning, besides their significance in connection with the delusion, a real, present meaning, as, for example, when she regrets that he did not succeed in confirming the Gradiva-gait on the street. "What a shame; perhaps you would not have needed to take the long journey here." (G. p. 69.) She learns also that he has named the bas-relief of her "Gradiva," and tells him that her real name is Zoë!

"The name suits you beautifully, but it sounds to me like bitter mockery, for 'Zoë' means 'life.'"

"One must adapt himself to the inevitable," she responds. "And I have long accustomed myself to being dead."

With the promise to be at the same place again on the morrow, she takes leave of him, after she has obtained the asphodel cluster. "To those who are more fortunate one gives roses in spring, but for me the flower of oblivion is the right one from your hand." (G. p. 70.) Melancholy is suited to one so long dead, who has now returned to life for a few short hours.

We begin now to understand and to hope. If the young lady, in whose form Gradiva is again revived, accepts Hanold's delusion so completely, she does it probably to free him from it. No other course is open; by opposition, one would destroy that possibility. Even the serious treatment of a real condition of this kind could proceed no differently than to place itself first on the ground story of the delusion-structure, and investigate it then as thoroughly as possible. If Zoë is the [129] right person, we shall soon learn how one cures delusions like those of our hero. We should also like to know how such a delusion originates. It would be very striking, and yet not without example and parallel, if the treatment and investigation of the delusion should coincide and, while it is being analysed, result in the explanation of its origin. We have a suspicion, of course, that our case might then turn out to be an "ordinary" love story, but one may not scorn love as a healing power for delusions; and was not our hero's captivation by the Gradiva-relief also a complete infatuation, directed, to be sure, at the past and lifeless?

After Gradiva's disappearance, there is heard once more a distant sound like the merry note of a bird flying over the city of ruins. The man who has remained behind picks up something white, which Gradiva has left, not a papyrus leaf, but a sketch-book with pencil drawings of Pompeii. We should say that the fact that she has forgotten the little book, in this place, is a pledge of her return, for we assert that one forgets nothing without a secret reason or a hidden motive.

The remainder of the day brings to our hero all sorts of remarkable discoveries and facts, which he neglects to fit together. In the wall of the portico where Gradiva disappeared, he notices to-day a narrow cleft, which is, however, wide enough to afford passage to an unusually slender figure. He recognizes the fact that Zoë-Gradiva does not need to sink into the ground here, an idea which is so senseless that he is now ashamed of the discarded belief, but that she uses this route to go back to her tomb. A faint shadow seems to 130him to dissolve at the end of the Street of Tombs, before the so-called Villa of Diomede. Dizzy, as on the previous day, and occupied with the same problem, he wanders now about Pompeii, wondering of what physical nature Zoë-Gradiva may be and whether one might feel anything if one touched her hand. A peculiar impulse urges him to undertake this experiment, and yet an equally great timidity in connection with the idea restrains him. On a hot, sunny slope he meets an older man who, from his equipment, must be a zoologist or a botanist, and seems to be busy catching things. The latter turns to him and says: "Are you interested in *Faraglionensis*? I should hardly have supposed it, but it seems thoroughly probable that they are found, not only in the *Faraglioni* of Capri, but also dwell permanently on the mainland. The method suggested by my colleague, Eimer, is really good; I have already used it often with the best of success. Please remain quite still." (*G.* p. 74.) The speaker stops talking then, and holds a little snare, made of a long grass-blade, before a narrow crevice, from which the blue, chatoyant, little head of a lizard peeps. Hanold leaves the lizard-hunter with the critical thought that it is hardly credible what foolishly remarkable purposes can cause people to make the long trip to Pompeii, in which criticism he does not, of course, include himself and his intention of seeking foot-prints of Gradiva in the ashes of Pompeii. The gentleman's face, moreover, seems familiar to him, as if he has noticed it casually in one of the two hotels; the man's manner of addressing him has also sounded as if directed at an acquaintance. As 131he continues his wandering, a side street leads him to a house not previously discovered by him; this proves to be the "Albergo del Sole." The hotel-keeper, who is not busy, avails himself of the opportunity to recommend highly his house and the excavated treasures in it. He asserts that he was present when there were found near the Forum the young lovers who, on realizing their inevitable destruction, had clasped each other in firm embrace and thus awaited death. Hanold has already heard of that before, and shrugged his shoulders over it, as a fabulous invention of some especially imaginative narrator, but to-day the words of the hotel-keeper awaken in him credulity, which soon stretches itself more when the former brings forth a metal brooch encrusted with green patina, which, in his presence, was gathered, with the remains of the girl, from the ashes. He secures this brooch without further critical consideration, and when, as he is leaving the hotel, he sees in an open window, nodding down, a cluster of white asphodel blossoms, the sight of the grave-flower thrills him as an attestation of the genuineness of his new possession.

With this brooch, however, a new delusion takes possession of him or, rather, the old one continues for a while, apparently not a good omen for the treatment which has been started. Not far from the Forum a couple of young lovers were excavated in an embrace, and in the dream he saw Gradiva lie down to sleep in that very neighbourhood, at the Apollo temple. Was it not possible that in reality she went still farther from the Forum to meet there some one with whom she then died?

A tormenting feeling, which we can perhaps 132compare to jealousy, originates from this supposition. He appeases it by referring to the uncertainty of the combination, and so far regains his senses as to be able to have his evening meal in "Hotel Diomed." His attention is attracted by two newly arrived guests, a man and a woman, whom, because of a certain resemblance, he considers brother and sister—in spite of the difference in the colour of their hair. They are the first people whom he has encountered on this trip who seem possibly congenial. A red Sorrento rose, which the young girl wears, awakes in him some memory—he cannot recall what. Finally he goes to bed and dreams; it is remarkable nonsense, but apparently concocted of the day's experiences. "Somewhere in the sun Gradiva sat making a trap out of a blade of grass, in order to catch a lizard, and she said,

'Please stay quite still—my colleague is right; the method is really good, and she has used it with greatest success!'" He resists the dream, even in his sleep, with the criticism that it is, of course, utter madness, and he succeeds in getting rid of it with the aid of an invisible bird, who utters a short, merry call and carries the lizard away in his beak.

In spite of all this ghostly visitation, he awakes rather cleared and settled mentally. A rose-bush, which bears flowers of the kind that he noticed yesterday on the young lady, recalls to him that in the night some one said that in the spring one gave roses. He plucks some of the roses involuntarily, and there must be some association with these which has a liberating effect upon his mind. Rid of his aversion to human beings, he takes the 133customary road to Pompeii, laden with the roses, the brooch and the sketch-book, and occupied by the different problems relating to Gradiva. The old delusion has become full of flaws; he already doubts if she is permitted to stay in Pompeii in the noon hour only, and not at other times. Emphasis, on that account, is transferred to the object recently acquired, and the jealousy connected with it torments him in all sorts of disguises. He might almost wish that the apparition should remain visible to only his eyes and escape the notice of others; in that way, he might consider her his exclusive property. During his ramble awaiting the noon hour he has a surprising encounter. In the Casa del Fauno he happens upon two people who doubtless believe themselves undiscoverable in a nook, for they are embracing each other and their lips meet. With amazement he recognizes in them the congenial couple of yesterday evening; but for brother and sister their present position, the embrace and the kiss are of too long duration. So it is a couple of lovers, probably a young bridal couple, another Augustus and Gretchen. Strange to relate, the sight of this now arouses in him nothing but pleasure, and fearful, as if he had disturbed a secret act of devotion, he withdraws unobserved. A deference which has long been lacking in him has been restored.

Arriving at Meleager's house, he is afraid that he may find Gradiva in the company of another man, and becomes so excited about it that he can find no other greeting for her than the question: "Are you alone?" With difficulty she makes him realize that he has picked the roses for her; 134he confesses to her the latest delusion, that she is the girl who was found in the Forum in her lover's embrace and to whom the green brooch had belonged. Not without mockery, she inquires if he found the piece in the sun. The latter—here called "Sole"— brings to light many things of that sort. As cure for the dizziness which he admits, she proposes to him to share a lunch with her and offers him half of a piece of white bread wrapped in tissue paper; the other half of this she consumes with apparent appetite. Thereat her faultless teeth gleam between her lips and, in biting the crust, cause a slight crunching sound. To her remark, "It seems to me as if we had already eaten our bread thus together once two thousand years ago. Can't you remember it?" (*G.* p. 88.) he cannot answer, but the strengthening of his mind by the nourishment, and all the evidences of present time in her do not fail to have effect on him. Reason stirs in him and makes him doubt the whole delusion that Gradiva is only a noonday ghost; on the other hand, there is the objection that she, herself, has just said that she had already shared her repast with him two thousand years ago. As a means of settling this conflict there occurs to him an experiment which he executes with slyness and restored courage. Her left hand, with its slender fingers, is resting on her knees, and one of the house-flies, about whose boldness and worthlessness he formerly became so indignant, alights on this hand. Suddenly Hanold's hand rises and claps, with no gentle stroke, on the fly and on Gradiva's hand. This bold experiment affords him twofold success: first the joyous conviction 135that he actually touched a really living, warm hand, then, however, a reprimand, before which he starts up in terror from his seat on the step. For from Gradiva's lips come the words, after she has recovered from her amazement, "You are surely apparently crazy, Norbert Hanold."

Calling a person by name is recognized as the best method of awakening him, when he is sleeping, or of awakening a somnambulist. Unfortunately we are not permitted to observe the results, for Norbert Hanold, of Gradiva's calling his name, which he had told to no one in Pompeii. For at this critical moment, the congenial lovers appear from the Casa del Fauno and the young lady calls, in a tone of pleasant surprise, "Zoë! You here, too? and

42

also on your honeymoon? You have not written me a word about it, you know." Before this new proof of the living reality of Gradiva, Hanold flees.

Zoë-Gradiva, too, is not most pleasantly surprised by the unexpected visit which disturbs her, it seems, in an important piece of work. Soon composed, she answers the question with a glib speech, in which she informs her friend, and especially us, about the situation; and thereby she knows how to get rid of the young couple. She extends her compliments, but she is not on her wedding-trip. "The young man who just went out is labouring also under a remarkable delusion; it seems to me that he believes a fly is buzzing in his head; well, every one has, of course, some kind of bee in his bonnet. As is my duty, I have some knowledge of entomology and can, therefore, be of a little service in such cases. My father [136]and I live in the 'Sole'; he, too, had a sudden and pleasing idea of bringing me here with him if I would be responsible for my own entertainment and make no demands upon him. I said to myself that I should certainly dig up something interesting alone here. Of course I had not reckoned at all on the find which I made—I mean the good fortune of meeting you, Gisa." (G. p. 92.) Zoë now feels obliged to leave at once, to be company for her father at the "Sole." So she goes, after she has introduced herself to us as the daughter of the zoologist and lizard-catcher, and has admitted in ambiguous words her therapeutic intentions and other secret ones. The direction which she takes is not that of the "Sun Hotel," in which her father is awaiting her, but it seems to her, too, that in the region of the Villa of Diomede a shadowy form is seeking its burial-place and disappears under one of the monuments; therefore, with foot poised each time almost perpendicularly, she directs her steps to the Street of Tombs. Thither, in shame and confusion, Hanold has fled, and is wandering up and down in the portico of the court without stopping, occupied with settling the rest of his problem by mental efforts. One thing has become unimpeachably clear to him; that he was utterly foolish and irrational to believe that he communed with a young Pompeiian girl who had become more or less physically alive again; and this clear insight into his madness forms incontestably an essential bit of progress in the return to sound reason. On the other hand, however, this living girl, with whom other people also communicate, as with one of a corporeal reality like theirs, is [137]Gradiva, and she knows his name; for the solution of this riddle his scarcely awakened reason is not strong enough. Emotionally, also, he is not calm enough to be equal to so difficult a task, for he would most gladly have been buried two thousand years ago in the Villa of Diomede, only to be sure of never meeting Zoë-Gradiva again. A violent longing to see her struggles meanwhile with the remnants of the inclination to flee, which has persisted in him.

Turning at one of the four corners of the colonnade, he suddenly recoils. On a fragmentary wall-ruin there sits one of the girls who met death here in the Villa of Diomede; but that attempt to take refuge again in the realm of madness is soon put aside; no, it is Gradiva, who has apparently come to give him the last bit of her treatment. She interprets rightly his first instinctive movement to flee, as an attempt to leave the place, and points out to him that he cannot escape, for outside a frightful cloudburst is in progress. The merciless girl begins the examination with the question as to what he intended in connection with the fly on her hand. He does not find courage to make use of a definite pronoun, but acquires the more valuable kind needed to put the deciding question.

"I was—as they say—somewhat confused mentally and ask pardon that I—the hand—in that way—how I could be so stupid, I can't understand—but I can't understand either how its owner could use my name in upbraiding me for my—my madness." (G. p. 98.)

"Your power of understanding has not yet progressed that far, Norbert Hanold. Of course, I [138]cannot be surprised, for you have long ago accustomed me to it. To make that discovery again, I should not have needed to come to Pompeii, and you could have confirmed it for me a good hundred miles nearer."

"A good hundred miles nearer; diagonally across from your house, in the corner house; in my window, in a cage, is a canary," she discloses to the still bewildered man.

This last word touches the hero like a memory from afar. That is surely the same bird whose song has suggested to him the trip to Italy.

"In that house lives my father, Richard Bertgang, professor of zoology."

As his neighbour, therefore, she is acquainted with him and his name. It seems as if the disappointment of a superficial solution is threatening us—a solution unworthy of our expectations.

As yet Norbert Hanold shows no regained independence of thought, when he repeats, "Then are you—are you Miss Zoë Bertgang? But she looked quite different——"

Miss Bertgang's answer shows then that other relations besides those of neighbourliness have existed between them. She knows how to intercede for the familiar manner of address, which he has, of course, used to the noonday spirit, but withdrawn again from the living girl; she makes former privileges of use to her here. "If you find that form of address more suitable between us, I can use it too, you know, but the other came to me more naturally. I don't know whether I looked different when we used to run about before with each other as friends, every day, and 139occasionally beat and cuffed each other for a change, but if, in recent years, you had favoured me with even one glance you might perhaps have seen that I have looked like this for a long time."

A childhood friendship had therefore existed between the two, perhaps a childhood love, from which the familiar form of address derived its justification. Isn't this solution perhaps as superficial as the one first supposed? The fact that it occurs to us that this childhood relation explains in an unexpected way so many details of what has occurred in the present intercourse between them makes the matter essentially deeper. Does it not seem that the blow on Zoë-Gradiva's hand which Norbert Hanold has so splendidly motivated by the necessity of solving, experimentally, the question of the physical existence of the apparition, is, from another standpoint, remarkably similar to a revival of the impulse for "beating and cuffing," whose sway in childhood Zoë's words have testified to? And when Gradiva puts to the archæologist the question whether it does not seem to him that they have once already, two thousand years ago, shared their luncheon, does not the incomprehensible question become suddenly senseful, when we substitute for the historical past the personal childhood, whose memories persist vividly for the girl, but seem to be forgotten by the young man? Does not the idea suddenly dawn upon us that the fancies of the young man about his Gradiva may be an echo of his childhood memories? Then they would, therefore, be no arbitrary products of his imagination, but determined, without his knowing it, by the existing 140material of childhood impressions already forgotten, but still active in him. We must be able to point out in detail the origin of these fancies, even if only by conjecture. If, for instance, Gradiva must be of pure Greek ancestry, the daughter of a respected man, perhaps of a priest of Ceres, that predisposes us fairly well for an after-effect of the knowledge of her Greek name—Zoë, and of her membership in the family of a professor of zoology. If, however, these fancies of Hanold's are transformed memories, we may expect to find in the disclosures of Zoë Bertgang, the suggestion of the sources of these fancies. Let us listen; she tells us of an intimate friendship of childhood; we shall soon learn what further development this childhood relation had in both.

"Then up to the time when people call us 'Backfisch,' for some unknown reason, I had really acquired a remarkable attachment for you, and thought that I could never find a more pleasing friend in the world. Mother, sister, or brother I had not, you know; to my father a slow-worm in alcohol was far more interesting than I, and people (I count girls such) must surely have something with which they can occupy their thoughts and the like. Then you were that something, but when archæology overcame you, I made the discovery that you—excuse the familiarity, but your new formality sounds absurd to me—I was saying that I imagined that you had become an intolerable person, who had no longer, at least for me, an eye in his head, a tongue in his mouth, nor any of the memories that I retained of our childhood friendship. So I probably looked 141different from what I did formerly, for when, occasionally, I met you at a party, even last winter, you did not look at me and I did not hear your voice; in this, of course, there was nothing that marked me out especially, for you treated all the others in the same way. To you I was but air, and you, with your shock of light hair, which I had formerly pulled so often, were as boresome, dry and tongue-tied as a stuffed cockatoo and at the same time as grandiose as an—archæopteryx; I believe the excavated antediluvian bird-monster is so called; but that your head harboured an imagination so magnificent as here in Pompeii to consider me as something excavated and restored to life—I had not surmised that of you, and when you suddenly stood before me unexpectedly, it cost me some effort at first to understand what kind of incredible fancy your imagination had invented. Then I was amused and, in spite of its madness, it was not entirely displeasing to me. For, as I said, I had not expected it of you." (*G.* p. 101.)

So she thus tells us clearly enough what, with the years, has become of the childhood friendship for both of them. With her it expanded into an intense love affair, for one must have something, you know, to which one, that is, a girl, pins her affections. Miss Zoë, the incarnation of cleverness and clarity, makes her psychic life, too, quite transparent for us. If it is already the general rule for a normal girl that she first turns her affection to her father, she is especially ready to do it, she who has no one but her father in her family; but this father has nothing left for her; the objects of science have captured all his interest. So she has to look around for another person, and clings with especial fervour to the playmate of her youth. When he, too, no longer has any eyes for her, it does not destroy her love, rather augments it, for he has become like her father, like him absorbed by science and, by it, isolated from life and from Zoë. So it is granted to her to be faithful in unfaithfulness, to find her father again in her beloved, to embrace both with the same feeling as we may say, to make them both identical in her emotions. Where do we get justification for this little psychological analysis, which may easily seem autocratic? In a single, but intensely characteristic detail the author of the romance gives it to us. When Zoë pictures for us the transformation of the playmate of her youth, which seems so sad for her, she insults him by a comparison with the archæopteryx, that bird-monster which belongs to the archæology of zoology. So she has found a single concrete expression for identifying the two people; her resentment strikes the beloved as well as the father with the same word. The archæopteryx is, so to speak, the compromise, or intermediary representation in which the folly of her beloved coincides with her thought of an analogous folly of her father.

With the young man, things have taken a different turn. The science of antiquity overcame him and left to him interest only in the women of bronze and stone. The childhood friendship died, instead of developing into a passion, and the memories of it passed into such absolute forgetfulness that he does not recognize nor pay any attention to the friend of his youth, when he meets her in society. Of course, when we continue our observations, we may doubt if "forgetfulness" is the right psychological term for the fate of these memories of our archæologist. There is a kind of forgetting which distinguishes itself by the difficulty with which the memory is awakened, even by strong objective appeals, as if a subjective resistance struggled against the revival. Such forgetting has received the name "repression" in psychopathology; the case which Jensen has presented to us seems to be an example of repression. Now we do not know, in general, whether, in psychic life, forgetting an impression is connected with the destruction of its memory-trace; about repression we can assert with certainty that it does not coincide with the destruction, the obliteration, of the memory. The repressed material cannot, as a rule, break through, of itself, as a memory, but remains potent and effective. Some day, under external influence, it causes psychic results which one may accept as products of transformation or as remnants of forgotten memories; and if one does not view them as such, they remain incomprehensible. In the fancies of Norbert Hanold about Gradiva, we thought we recognized already the remnants of the repressed memories of his childhood friendship with Zoë Bertgang. Quite legitimately one may expect such a recurrence of the repressed material, if the man's erotic feelings cling to the repressed ideas, if his erotic life has been involved in the repression. Then there is truth in the old Latin proverb which was perhaps originally aimed at expulsion through external influences, not at inner conflict: "You may drive out natural disposition with a two-pronged fork, but it will always return," but it does not tell all, announces only the fact of the recurrence of repressed material, and does not describe at all the most remarkable manner of this recurrence, which is accomplished as if by malicious treason; the very thing which has been chosen as a means of repression—like the "two-pronged fork" of the proverb—becomes the carrier of the thing recurring; in and behind the agencies of repression the material repressed finally asserts itself victoriously. A well-known etching by Félicien Rops illustrates this fact, which is generally overlooked and lacks acceptance, more impressively than many explanations could; and he does it in the typical case of the repression in the lives of saints and penitents. From the temptations of the world, an ascetic monk has sought refuge in the image of the crucified Saviour. Then, phantom-like, this cross sinks and, in its stead, there rises shining, the image of a voluptuous, unclad woman, in the same position of the crucifixion. Other painters of less psychological insight have, in such representations of temptation, depicted sin as bold and triumphant, near the Saviour on the cross. Rops, alone, has allowed it to take the place of the Saviour on the cross; he seems to have known that the thing repressed proceeds, at its recurrence, from the agency of repression itself.

If Norbert Hanold were a living person, who had, by means of archæology, driven love and the memory of his childhood friendship out of 145his life, it would now be legitimate and correct that an antique relief should awaken in him the forgotten memory of the girl beloved in his childhood; it would be his well-deserved fate to have fallen in love with the stone representation of Gradiva, behind which, by virtue of an unexplained resemblance, the living and neglected Zoë becomes effective.

Miss Zoë, herself, seems to share our conception of the delusion of the young archæologist, for the pleasure which she expresses at the end of her "unreserved, detailed and instructive lecture" is hardly based on anything other than her readiness to refer his entire interest in Gradiva to her person. This is exactly what she does not believe him capable of, and what, in spite of all the disguises of the delusion, she recognizes as such. Her psychic treatment of him has a beneficent effect; he feels himself free, as the delusion is now replaced by that of which it can be only a distorted and unsatisfactory copy. He immediately remembers and recognizes her as his good, cheerful, clever comrade who has not changed essentially; but he finds something else most strange—

"That a person must die to become alive again," says the girl, "but for archæologists that is of course necessary." (G. p. 102.) She has apparently not yet pardoned him for the détour which he made from the childhood friendship through the science of antiquity to this relation which has recently been established.

"No, I mean your name—Because Bertgang has the same meaning as Gradiva and signifies 'the one splendid in walking.'" (G. p. 102.)

146Even we are not prepared for that. Our hero begins to rise from his humility and to play an active rôle. He is, apparently, entirely cured of his delusion, lifted far above it, and proves this by tearing asunder the last threads of the web of delusion. Patients, also, who have been freed from the compulsion of their delusion, by the disclosure of the repression behind it, always act in just that way. When they have once understood, they themselves offer the solutions for the last and most significant riddles of their strange condition in suddenly emerging ideas. We had already believed, of course, that the Greek ancestry of the mythical Gradiva was an after-effect of the Greek name, Zoë, but with the name, Gradiva, we had ventured nothing; we had supposed it the free creation of Norbert Hanold's imagination, and behold! this very name now shows itself to be a remnant, really a translation of the repressed family-name of the supposedly forgotten beloved of his youth.

The derivation and solution of the delusion are now completed. What follows may well serve as a harmonious conclusion of the tale. In regard to the future, it can have only a pleasant effect on us, if the rehabilitation of the man, who formerly had to play the lamentable rôle of one needing to be cured, progresses, and he succeeds in awakening in the girl some of the emotions which he formerly experienced. Thus it happens that he makes her jealous by mentioning the congenial young lady, who disturbed them in Meleager's house, and by the acknowledgment that the latter was the first girl who had impressed him much. 147When Zoë is then about to take a cool departure, with the remark that now everything is reasonable again, she herself not least of all, that he might look up Gisa Hartleben, or whatever her name might now be, and be of scientific assistance to her about the purpose of her stay in Pompeii, but she has to go now to the "Albergo del Sole" where her father is already waiting for her at lunch, perhaps they may see each other again some time at a party in Germany or on the moon, he seizes upon the troublesome fly as a means of taking possession of her cheek, first, and then of her lips, and assumes the aggressive, which is the duty of a man in the game of love. Only once more does a shadow seem to fall on their happiness, when Zoë reminds him that now she must really go to her father, who will otherwise starve in the "Sole." "Your father—what will he——?" (G. p. 106.)

46

But the clever girl knows how to silence the apprehension quickly. "Probably he will do nothing; I am not an indispensable piece in his zoological collection; if I were, my heart would probably not have clung to you so unwisely." Should the father, however, by way of exception, in this case, have an opinion different from hers, there is a sure method. Hanold needs only to go over to Capri, there catch a *lacerta faraglionensis*, for which purpose he may practise the technique on her little finger, then set the animal free again here, catch it before the eyes of the zoologist and give him the choice of the *faraglionensis* on the mainland or his daughter, a proposal in which mockery, as one may easily note, is combined with bitterness, an admonition to the betrothed, 148also, not to follow too closely the model after which his beloved has chosen him. Norbert Hanold sets us at rest on this matter, as he expresses, by all sorts of apparently trivial symptoms, the great transformation which has come over him. He voices the intention of taking a wedding trip with his Zoë to Italy and Pompeii, as if he had never been indignant at the newly married travellers, Augustus and Gretchen. His feelings towards this happy couple, who so unnecessarily travelled more than one hundred miles from their German home, have entirely disappeared from his memory. Certainly the author is right when he cites such weakening of memory as the most valuable mark of a mental change. Zoë replies to the announced desire about the destination of their journey, "*by her childhood friend who had, in a way, also been excavated from the ashes,*" (G. p. 108), that she does not yet feel quite alive enough for such geographical decision.

Beautiful reality has now triumphed over the delusion. Yet an honour still awaits the latter before the two leave Pompeii. When they have arrived at the Hercules Gate, where, at the beginning of the Strada Consolare, old stepping-stones cross the street, Norbert Hanold stops and asks the girl to go ahead. She understands him and, "raising her dress slightly with her left hand, Gradiva *rediviva* Zoë Bertgang, viewed by him with dreamily observing eyes, crossed with her calmly buoyant walk, through the sunlight, over the stepping-stones." With the triumph of eroticism, what was beautiful and valuable in the delusion is now acknowledged.

149With the last comparison of "the childhood friend excavated from the ashes," the author of the story has, however, put into our hand the key of the symbolism which the delusion of the hero made use of in the disguise of the repressed memory. There is no better analogy for repression, which at the same time makes inaccessible and conserves something psychic, than the burial which was the fate of Pompeii, and from which the city was able to arise again through work with the spade. Therefore in his imagination the young archæologist had to transport to Pompeii the original figure of the relief which reminded him of the forgotten beloved of his youth. Jensen, however, had a good right to linger over the significant resemblance which his fine sense traced out between a bit of psychic occurrence in the individual and a single historical event in the history of man.

150

II

It was really our intention to investigate with the aid of definite analytic method only the two or three dreams which are found in the tale *Gradiva*; how did it happen then that we allowed ourselves to be carried away with the analysis of the whole story and the examination of the psychic processes of the two chief characters? Well, that was no superfluous work, but a necessary preparation. Even when we wish to understand the real dreams of an actual person, we must concern ourselves intensively with the character and the fortunes of this person, not only the experiences shortly before the dream, but also those of the remote past. I think, however, that we are not yet free to turn to our real task, but must still linger over the piece of fiction itself, and perform more preparatory work.

Our readers will, of course, have noticed with surprise that till now we have considered Norbert Hanold and Zoë Bertgang in all their psychic expressions and activities, as if they were real individuals and not creatures of an author, as if the mind of their creator were absolutely transparent, not a refractory and cloudy medium; and our procedure must seem all the more surprising when the author of *Gradiva* expressly disavows 151the portrayal of reality by calling his tale a "Fancy." We find, however, that all his pictures copy reality so faithfully that we should not contradict if *Gradiva* were called not a "Fancy," but a study in psychiatry. Only in two points has Wilhelm Jensen made use of his license, to create suppositions which do not seem to have roots in the earth of actual law: first, when he has the young archæologist find a genuinely antique bas-relief which, not only in the detail of the position of the foot in walking, but in all details, the shape of the face, and the bearing, copies a person living much later, so that he can consider the physical manifestation of this person to be the cast endowed with life; second, when the hero is caused to meet the living girl in Pompeii, whither his fancy has transported the dead girl, while he separates himself, by the journey to Pompeii, from the living girl, whom he has noticed on the street of his home city; this second instance is no tremendous deviation from the possibilities of life; it asks aid only of chance, which undeniably plays a part in so many human fates, and, moreover, makes it reasonable, for this chance reflects again the destiny which has decreed that through flight one is delivered over to the very thing that one is fleeing from. More fantastic, and originating solely in the author's arbitrariness, seems the first supposition which brings in its train the detailed resemblance of the cast to the living girl, where moderation might have limited the conformity to the one trait of the position of the foot in walking. One might then have tried to let one's own imagination play in order to establish connection 152with reality. The name Bertgang might point to the fact that the women of that family had been distinguished, even in ancient times, by the characteristic of a beautiful gait, and by heredity the German Bertgang was connected with those Romans, a woman of whose family had caused the ancient artist to fix in a bas-relief the peculiarity of her walk. As the individual variations of human structure are, however, not independent of one another, and as the ancient types, which we come upon in the collections, are actually always emerging again in our midst, it would not be entirely impossible that a modern Bertgang should repeat again the form of her ancient forbear, even in all the other traits of her physique. Inquiry of the author of the story for the sources of this creation might well be wiser than such speculation; a good prospect of solving again a bit of supposed arbitrariness would probably then appear. As, however, we have not access to the psychic life of the author, we leave to him the undiminished right of building up a thoroughly valid development on an improbable supposition, a right which Shakespeare, for example, has asserted in *King Lear.*

Otherwise, we wish to repeat, Wilhelm Jensen has given us an absolutely correct study in psychiatry, in which we may measure our understanding of psychic life, a story of illness and cure adapted to the inculcation of certain fundamental teachings of medical psychology. Strange enough that he should have done this! What if, in reply to questioning, he should deny this intention? It is so easy to draw comparisons and to put constructions on 153things. Are we not rather the ones who have woven secret meanings, which were foreign to him, into the beautiful poetic tale? Possibly; we shall come back to that later. As a preliminary, however, we have tried to refrain from interpretations with that tendency, by reproducing the story, in almost every case, from the very words of the writer; and we have had him furnish text as well as commentary, himself. Any one who will compare our text with that of *Gradiva* will have to grant this.

Perhaps in the judgment of the majority we are doing a poor service for him when we declare his work a study in psychiatry. An author is to avoid all contact with psychiatry, we are told, and leave to physicians the portrayal of morbid psychic conditions. In reality no true author has ever heeded this commandment. The portrayal of the psychic life of human beings is, of course, his most especial domain; he was always the precursor of science and of scientific psychology. The borderline between normal and morbid psychic conditions is, in a way, a conventional one, and, in another way, in such a state of flux that probably every one of us oversteps it many times in the course of a day. On the other hand, psychiatry would do wrong to wish to limit itself continually to the study of those serious and cloudy illnesses which arise from rude disturbances of the delicate psychic apparatus. It has no less interest in the lesser and adjustable deviations from the normal which we cannot yet trace back farther than disturbances in the play of psychic forces; indeed, it is by means of these that it can understand 154normal conditions, as well as the manifestations of serious illness. Thus the author cannot yield to the psychiatrist nor the psychiatrist to the author, and the poetic treatment of a theme from psychiatry may result correctly without damage to beauty.

The imaginative representation of the story of illness and its treatment, which we can survey better after finishing the story and relieving our own suspense, is really correct. Now we wish to reproduce it with the technical expressions of our science, in doing which it will not be necessary to repeat what has already been related.

Norbert Hanold's condition is called a "delusion" often enough by the author of the story, and we also have no reason to reject this designation. We can mention two chief characteristics of "delusion," by which it is not, of course, exhaustively described, but is admittedly differentiated from other disturbances. It belongs first to that group of illnesses which do not directly affect the physical, but express themselves only by psychic signs, and it is distinguished secondly by the fact that "fancies" have assumed control, that is, are believed and have acquired influence on actions. If we recall the journey to Pompeii to seek in the ashes the peculiarly-formed foot-prints of Gradiva, we have in it a splendid example of an act under the sway of the delusion. The psychiatrist would perhaps assign Norbert Hanold's delusion to the great group of paranoia and designate it as a "fetichistic erotomania," because falling in love with the bas-relief would be the most striking thing to him and because, to his conception, which 155coarsens everything, the interest of the young archæologist in the feet and foot-position of women must seem suspiciously like fetichism. All such names and divisions of the different kinds of delusion are, however, substantially useless and awkward.[2]

The old-school psychiatrist would, moreover, stamp our hero as a dégénéré, because he is a person capable, on account of such strange predilections, of developing a delusion, and would investigate the heredity which has unrelentingly driven him to such a fate. In this, however, Jensen does not follow him; with good reason, he brings us nearer to the hero to facilitate for us æsthetic sympathy with him; with the diagnosis "dégénéré," whether or not it may be justifiable to us scientifically, the young archæologist is at once moved farther from us, for we, readers, are, of course, normal people and the measure of humanity. The essential facts of heredity and constitution in connection with this condition also concern the author of *Gradiva* little; instead, he is engrossed in the personal, psychic state which can give rise to such a delusion.

In an important point, Norbert Hanold acts quite differently from ordinary people. He has no interest in the living woman; science, which he serves, has taken this interest from him and transferred it to women of stone or bronze. Let us not consider this an unimportant peculiarity; it is really the basis of the story, for one day it happens that a single such bas-relief claims for itself all 156the interest which would otherwise belong only to the living woman, and thereby originates the delusion. Before our eyes there is then unfolded the story of how this delusion is cured by a fortunate set of circumstances, the interest transferred back again from the cast to the living girl. The author of the story does not allow us to trace the influences because of which our hero begins to avoid women; he only suggests to us that such conduct is not explained by his predisposition which is invested with a rather fanciful— we might add, erotic—need. We learn later also that in his childhood he did not avoid other children; he was then friendly with the little girl, was inseparable from her, shared with her his lunches, cuffed her, and was pulled around by her. In such attachment, such a combination of tenderness and aggression, is expressed the incomplete eroticism of child life, which expresses its activities first spitefully and then irresistibly and which, during childhood, only physicians and writers usually recognize as eroticism. Our author gives us to understand clearly that he has those intentions, for he suddenly causes to awaken in his hero, with suitable motive, a lively interest in the gait and foot-position of women, an interest which, in science, as well as among the ladies of his home-city, must bring him into disrepute as a foot-fetichist, and is to us, however, necessarily derived from the memory of his childhood playmate. The girl, to be sure, was characterized, as a child, by the beautiful walk with her foot almost perpendicular as she stepped out, and through the portrayal of this very gait an antique bas-relief 157later acquired for Norbert Hanold great significance. Let us add, moreover, immediately, that the author of *Gradiva* stands in complete agreement with science in regard to the derivation of the remarkable manifestation of fetichism. Since the investigations by Binet we really try to trace fetichism back to erotic impressions of childhood.

The condition of continued avoidance of women gives the personal qualification, as we say, the disposition for the formation of a delusion; the development of psychic disturbance begins at the moment when a chance impression awakens the forgotten childhood experiences which are emphasized in an erotic way that is at least traceable. Awakened is really not the right term, however, when we consider the further results. We must reproduce our author's correct representation in a mode of expression artistically correct, and psychological. On seeing the relief Norbert Hanold does not remember that he has seen such a foot-position in the friend of his youth; he certainly does not remember and yet every effect of the relief proceeds from such connection with the impression of his childhood. The childhood-impression, stirred, becomes active, so that it begins to show activity, though it does not appear in consciousness, but remains "unconscious," a term which we now use unavoidably in psychopathology. This term "unconscious" we should now like to see withdrawn from all the conflicts of philosophers and natural philosophers, which have only etymological significance. For psychic processes which are active and yet at the same time do not come through into the consciousness 158of the person referred to, we have at present no better name and we mean nothing else by "unconsciousness." If many thinkers wish to dispute as unreasonable the existence of such an unconscious, we think they have never busied themselves with analogous psychic phenomena, and are under the spell of the common idea that everything psychic which is active and intensive becomes, thereby, at the same time, conscious, and they have still to learn what our author knows very well, that there are, of course, psychic processes, which, in spite of the fact that they are intensive and show energetic activities, remain far removed from consciousness.

We said once that the memories of the childhood relations with Zoë are in a state of "repression" with Norbert Hanold; and we have called them "unconscious memories." Here we must, of course, turn our attention to the relation between the two technical terms which seem to coincide in meaning. It is not hard to clear this up. "Unconscious" is the broader term, "repressed" the narrower. Everything that is repressed is unconscious; but we cannot assert that everything unconscious is repressed. If Hanold, at the sight of the relief, had remembered his Zoë's manner of walking, then a formerly unconscious memory would have become immediately active and conscious, and thus would have shown that it was not formerly repressed. "Unconscious" is a purely descriptive term, in many respects indefinite and, so to speak, static; "repressed" is a dynamic expression which takes into consideration the play of psychic forces and the fact that there is present an effort to express all psychic activities, among them that of becoming 159conscious again, but also a counterforce, a resistance, which might hinder a part of these psychic activities, among these, also, getting into consciousness. The mark of the repressed material is that, in spite of its intensity, it cannot break through into consciousness. In Hanold's case, therefore, it was a matter, at the appearance of the bas-relief on his horizon, of a repressed unconscious, in short of a repression.

The memories of his childhood association with the girl who walks beautifully are repressed in Norbert Hanold, but this is not yet the correct view of the psychological situation. We remain on the surface so long as we treat only of memories and ideas. The only valuable things in psychic life are, rather, the emotions. All psychic powers are significant only through their fitness to awaken emotions. Ideas are repressed only because they are connected with liberations of emotions, which are not to come to light; it would be more correct to say that repression deals with the emotions, but these are comprehensible to us only in connection with ideas. Thus, in Norbert Hanold, the erotic feelings are repressed, and, as his eroticism neither knows nor has known another object than Zoë Bertgang of his youth, the memories of her are forgotten. The antique bas-relief awakens the slumbering eroticism in him and makes the childhood memories active. On account of a resistance in him to the eroticism, these memories can become active only as unconscious. What now happens in him is a struggle between the power of eroticism and the forces that are repressing it; the result of this struggle is a delusion.

160Our author has omitted to give the motive whence originates the repression of the erotic life in his hero; the latter's interest in science is, of course, only the means of which the repression makes use; the physician would have to probe deeper here, perhaps in this case without finding the foundation. Probably, however, the author of *Gradiva*, as we have admiringly emphasized, has not hesitated to represent to us how the awakening of the repressed eroticism results from the very sphere of the means which are serving the repression. It is rightly an antique, the bas-relief of a woman, through which our archæologist is snatched and admonished out of his alienation from love to pay the debt with which we are charged by our birth.

The first manifestations of the process now stimulated by the bas-relief are fancies which play with the person represented by it. The model appears to him to be something "of the present," in the best sense, as if the artist had fixed the girl walking on the street from life. The name, Gradiva, which he forms from the epithet of the war-god advancing to battle, Mars Gradivus, he lends to the ancient girl; with more and more definitions he endows her with a personality. She may be the daughter of an esteemed man, perhaps of a patrician, who is associated with the temple service of a divinity; he believes that he reads Greek ancestry in her features, and finally this forces him to transport her far from the confusion of a metropolis to more peaceful Pompeii, where he has her walking over the lava stepping-stones which make possible the crossing of the street. 161 These feats of fancy seem arbitrary enough and yet again harmlessly unsuspicious. Even when from them is produced, for the first time, the impulse to act, when the archæologist, oppressed by the problem whether such foot-position corresponds to reality, begins observations from life, in looking at the feet of contemporary women and girls, this act covers itself by conscious, scientific motives, as if all the interest in the bas-relief of Gradiva had originated in his professional interest in archæology. The women and girls on the street, whom he uses as objects for his investigation, must, of course, assume a different, coarsely erotic conception of his conduct, and we must admit that they are right. For us, there is no doubt that Hanold knows as little about his motives as about the origin of his fancies concerning Gradiva. These latter are, as we shall learn later, echoes of his memories of the beloved of his youth, remnants of these memories, transformations and disfigurements of them, after they have failed to push into consciousness in unchanged form. The so-called æsthetic judgment that the relief represents "something of the present" is substituted for the knowledge that such a gait belongs to a girl known to him and crossing streets *in the present*; behind the impression "from life" and the fancy about her Greek traits, is hidden the memory of her name, Zoë, which, in Greek, means *life*; Gradiva is, as the man finally cured of the delusion tells us, a good translation of her family-name, Bertgang, which means *splendid or magnificent in walking*; the decisions about her father arise from the knowledge that Zoë Bertgang is the daughter of an 162 esteemed university instructor, which is probably translated into the antique as temple service. Finally his imagination transports her to Pompeii not "because her calm, quiet manner seems to require it," but because, in his science, he has found no other nor better analogy to the remarkable condition in which he has traced out, by vague reconnoitring, his memories of his childhood friendship. If he once covered up what was so close to him, his own childhood, with the classic past, then the burial of Pompeii, this disappearance, with the preservation of the past, offers a striking resemblance to the *repression* of which he has knowledge by means of so-called "endopsychic" perceptions. The same symbolism, therefore, which the author has the girl use consciously at the end of the tale, is working in him.

"I said to myself that I should certainly dig up something interesting alone here. Of course, I had not reckoned at all on the find which I made." (*G.* p. 92.) At the end (*G.* p. 108), the girl answers to the announced desire about the destination of their journey, "by her childhood friend who had, in a way, also been excavated from the ashes."

Thus we find at the very beginning of the performances of Hanold's fancies and actions, a twofold determination, a derivation from two different sources. One determination is the one which appears to Hanold, himself; the other, the one which discloses itself to us upon re-examination of his psychic processes. One, the conscious one, is related to the person of Hanold; the other is the one entirely unconscious to him. One originates 163 entirely from the series of associations connected with archæological science; the other, however, proceeds from the repressed memories which have become active in him, and the emotional impulses attached to them. The one seems superficial, and covers up the other, which masks itself behind the former. One might say that the scientific motivation serves the unconscious eroticism as cloak, and that science has placed itself completely at the service of the delusion, but one may not forget, either, that the unconscious determination can effect nothing but what is at the time satisfactory to the scientific conscious. The symptoms of delusion—fancies as well as acts—are results of a compromise between two psychic streams, and in a compromise the demands of each of the two parties are considered; each party has been obliged to forego something that he wished to carry out. Where a compromise has been established, there was a struggle, here the conflict assumed by us between the suppressed eroticism and the forces which keep it alive in the repression. In the formation of a delusion this struggle is never ended.

Attack and resistance are renewed after every compromise-formation, which is, so to speak, never fully satisfactory. This our author also knows and therefore he causes a feeling of discontent, a peculiar restlessness, to dominate his hero in this phase of the disturbance, as preliminary to and guarantee of further developments.

These significant peculiarities of the twofold determination for fancies and decisions, of the formation of conscious pretexts for actions, for 164the motivation of which the repressed has given the greater contribution, will, in the further progress of the story, occur to us oftener, and perhaps more clearly; and this rightfully, for in this Jensen has grasped and represented the never-failing, chief characteristic of the morbid psychic processes. The development of Norbert Hanold's delusion progresses in a dream, which, caused by no new event, seems to proceed entirely from his psychic life, which is occupied by a conflict. Yet let us stop before we proceed to test whether the author of *Gradiva*, in the formation of his dreams, meets our expectation of a deeper understanding. Let us first ask what psychiatry has to say about his ideas of the origin of a delusion, how it stands on the matter of the rôle of repression and the unconscious, of conflict and compromise-formation. Briefly, can our author's representation of the genesis of a delusion stand before the judgment of science?

And here we must give the perhaps unexpected answer that, unfortunately, matters are here actually just reversed; science does not stand before the accomplishment of our author. Between the essential facts of heredity and constitution, and the seemingly complete creations of delusion, there yawns a breach which we find filled up by the writer of *Gradiva*. Science does not yet recognize the significance of repression nor the fact that it needs the unconscious for explanation to the world of psychopathological phenomena; it does not seek the basis of delusion in psychic conflict, and does not regard its symptoms as a compromise-formation. Then our author stands alone against 165all science? No, not that— if the present writer may reckon his own works as science. For he, himself, has for some years interceded—and until recently almost alone[3]—for the views which he finds here in *Gradiva* by W. Jensen, and he has presented them in technical terms. He has pointed out exhaustively, for the conditions known as hysteria and obsession, the suppression of impulses and the repression of the ideas, through which the suppressed impulse is represented, as a characteristic condition of psychic disturbance, and he has repeated the same view soon afterwards for many kinds of delusion.[4] Whether the impulses which are, for this reason, considered are always components of the sex-impulse, or might be of a different nature, is a problem of indifference in the analysis of *Gradiva*, as, in the case chosen by the author, it is a matter only of the suppression of the erotic feeling. The views concerning psychic conflict, and the formation of symptoms by compromises between the two psychic forces which are struggling with each other, the present writer has found valid in cases professionally treated and actually observed, in exactly the same way that he was able to observe it in Norbert Hanold, the invention of our author.[5] The tracing back of neurotic, especially of hysterically morbid activities 166to the influence of unconscious thoughts, P. Janet, the pupil of the great Charcot, had undertaken before the present writer, and in conjunction with Josef Breuer in Vienna.[6]

It had actually occurred to the present writer, when, in the years following 1893, he devoted himself to investigations of the origin of psychic disturbances, to seek confirmation of his results from authors, and therefore it was no slight surprise to him to learn that in *Gradiva*, published in 1903, an author gave to his creation the very foundation which the former supposed that he, himself, was finding authority for, as new, from his experiences as a physician. How did the author come upon the same knowledge as the physician, at least upon a procedure which would suggest that he possessed it?

Norbert Hanold's delusion, we said, acquires further development through a dream, which he has in the midst of his efforts to authenticate a gait like Gradiva's in the streets of his home-city. The content of this dream we can outline briefly. The dreamer is in Pompeii on that day which brought destruction to the unfortunate city, experiences the horrors without himself getting into danger, suddenly sees Gradiva walking there and immediately understands, as quite natural, that, as she is, of course, a Pompeiian, she is living in her native city and "without his having any suspicion of it, was his contemporary." He is 167seized with fear for her, calls to her, whereupon she turns her face toward him momentarily. Yet she walks on without heeding him at all, lies down on the steps of the Apollo temple, and is buried by the rain of ashes, after her face has changed colour as if it were turning to white marble, until it completely resembles a bas-relief. On awakening, he interprets the noise of the metropolis, which reaches his ear, as the cries for help of the desperate inhabitants of Pompeii and the booming of the turbulent sea. The feeling that what he has dreamed has really happened to him persists for some time after his awakening, and the conviction that Gradiva lived in Pompeii and died on that fatal day remains from this dream as a new, supplementary fact for his delusion.

It is less easy for us to say what the author of *Gradiva* intended by this dream, and what caused him to connect the development of this delusion directly with a dream. Assiduous investigation of dreams has, to be sure, gathered enough examples of the fact that mental disturbance is connected with and proceeds from dreams,[7] and even in the life-history of certain eminent men, impulses for important deeds and decisions are said to have been engendered by dreams; but our comprehension does not gain much by these analogies; let us hold, therefore, to our case, the case of the archæologist, Norbert Hanold, a fiction of our author. At which end must one lay hold of such a dream to introduce meaning into it, if it is not to remain an unnecessary adornment of fiction? 168I can imagine that the reader exclaims at this place: "The dream is, of course, easy to explain—a simple anxiety-dream, caused by the noise of the metropolis, which is given the new interpretation of the destruction of Pompeii, by the archæologist busied with his Pompeiian girl!" On account of the commonly prevailing disregard of the activities of dreams, one usually limits the demands for dream-explanations so that one seeks for a part of the dream-content an external excitation which covers itself by means of the content. This external excitation for the dream would be given by the noise which wakens the sleeper; the interest in this dream would be thereby terminated. Would that we had even one reason to suppose that the metropolis had been noisier than usual on this morning! If, for example, our author had not omitted to inform us that Hanold had that night, contrary to his custom, slept by an open window! What a shame that our author didn't take the trouble! And if an anxiety-dream were only so simple a thing! No, this interest is not terminated in so simple a way.

The connection with the external, sensory stimulus is not at all essential for the dream-formation. The sleeper can neglect this excitation from the outer world; he may be awakened by it without forming a dream, he may also weave it into his dream, as happens here, if it is of no use to him from any other motive; and there is an abundance of dreams for whose content such a determination by a sensory excitation of the sleeper cannot be shown. No, let us try another way.

Perhaps we can start from the residue which 169the dream leaves in Hanold's waking life. It had formerly been his fancy that Gradiva was a Pompeiian. Now this assumption becomes a certainty and the second certainty is added that she was buried there in the year 79.[8] Sorrowful feelings accompany this progress of the formation of the delusion like an echo of the fear which had filled the dream. This new grief about Gradiva will seem to us not exactly comprehensible; Gradiva would now have been dead for many centuries even if she had been saved in the year 79 from destruction. Or ought one to be permitted to squabble thus with either Norbert Hanold or his creator? Here, too, no way seems to lead to explanation. We wish, nevertheless, to remark that a very painful, emotional stress clings to the augmentation which the delusion derives from this dream.

Otherwise, however, our perplexity is not dispelled. This dream does not explain itself; we must decide to borrow from *Traumdeutung* by the present writer, and to use some of the rules given there for the solution of dreams.

One of these rules is that a dream is regularly connected with the day before the dream. Our author seems to wish to intimate that he has followed this rule by connecting the dream directly with Hanold's "pedestrian investigations." Now the latter means nothing but a search for Gradiva whom he expects to recognize by her characteristic manner of walking. The dream ought, therefore, to contain a reference to where Gradiva is to be found. It really does contain it by showing her in Pompeii, but that is no news for us.

170Another rule says: If, after the dream, the reality of the dream-pictures continues unusually long so that one cannot free himself from the dream, this is not a kind of mistake in judgment called forth by the vividness of the dream-pictures, but is a psychic act in itself, an assurance which refers to the dream-content, that something in it is as real as it has been dreamed to be, and one is right to believe this assurance. If we stop at these two rules, we must decide that the dream gives real information about the whereabouts of Gradiva, who is being sought. We now know Hanold's dream; does the application of these two rules lead to any sensible meaning?

Strange to say, yes. This meaning is disguised only in a special way so that one does not recognize it immediately. Hanold learns in the dream that the girl sought lives in the city and in his own day. That is, of course, true of Zoë Bertgang, only that in his dream the city is not the German university-city, but Pompeii, the time not the present, but the year 79, according to our reckoning. It is a kind of disfigurement by displacement; not Gradiva is transported to the present, but the dreamer to the past; but we are also given the essential and new fact *that he shares locality and time with the girl sought*. Whence, then, this dissimulation and disguise which must deceive us as well as the dreamer about the peculiar meaning and content of the dream? Well, we have already means at hand to give us a satisfactory answer to this question.

Let us recall all that we have heard about the nature and origin of fancies, these preliminaries of 171delusion. They are substitution for and remnants of different repressed memories, which a resistance does not allow to push into consciousness, which, however, become conscious by heeding the censor of resistance, by means of transformations and disfigurements. After this compromise is completed, the former memories have become fancies, which may easily be misunderstood by the conscious person, that is, may be understood to be the ruling psychic force. Now let us suppose that the dream-pictures are the so-called physiological delusion-products of a man, the compromise-results of that struggle between what is repressed and what is dominant, which exist probably even in people absolutely normal in the daytime. Then we understand that we have to consider the dream something disfigured behind which there is to be sought something else, not disfigured, but, in a sense, something offensive, like Hanold's repressed memories behind his fancies. One expresses the admitted opposition by distinguishing what the dreamer remembers on waking, as *manifest dream-content*, from what formed the basis of the dream before the censor's disfigurement, *the latent dream-thoughts*. To interpret a dream, then, means to translate the manifest dream-content into the latent dream-thoughts, which make retrogressive the disfigurement that had to be approved by the resistance censor. When we turn these deliberations to the dream which is occupying us, we find that the latent dream-thoughts must have been as follows: "The girl who has that beautiful walk, whom you are seeking, lives really in this city with you;" but in this form the thought could 172not become conscious; in its way there stood the fact that a fancy had established, as a result of a former compromise, the idea that Gradiva was a Pompeiian girl, and therefore nothing remained, if the actual fact of her living in the same locality and at the same time was to be perceived, but to assume the disfigurement: you are living in Pompeii at the time of Gradiva; and this then is the idea which the manifest dream-content realizes and represents as a present time which he is living in.

A dream is rarely the representation, one might say the staging, of a single thought, but generally of a number of them, a web of thoughts. In Hanold's dream there is conspicuous another component of the content, whose disfigurement is easily put aside so that one may learn the latent idea represented by it. This is the end of the dream to which the assurance of reality can also be extended. In the dream the beautiful walker, Gradiva, is transformed into a bas-relief. That is, of course, nothing but an ingenious and poetic representation of the actual procedure. Hanold had, indeed, transferred his interest from the living girl to the bas-relief; the beloved had been transformed into a stone relief. The latent dream-thoughts, which remain unconscious, wish to transform the relief back into the living girl; in connection with the foregoing they speak to him somewhat as follows: "You are, of course, interested in the bas-relief of Gradiva only because it reminds you of the present, here-living Zoë." But this insight would mean the end of the delusion, if it could become conscious.

Is it our duty to substitute unconscious thoughts 173thus for every single bit of the manifest dream-content? Strictly speaking, yes; in the interpretation of a dream which had actually been dreamed, we should not be allowed to avoid this duty. The dreamer would then have to give us an exhaustive account. It is easily understood that we cannot enforce such a demand in connection with the creature of our author; we will not, however, overlook the fact that we have not yet submitted the chief content of this dream to the work of interpretation and translation.

Hanold's dream is, of course, an anxiety-dream. Its content is fearful; anxiety is felt by the dreamer in sleep, and painful feelings remain after it. That is not of any great help for our attempt at explanation; we are again forced to borrow largely from the teachings of dream-interpretation. This admonishes us not to fall into the error of deriving the fear that is felt in a dream from the content of a dream, not to use the dream-content like the content of ideas of waking life. It calls to our attention how often we dream the most horrible things without feeling any trace of fear. Rather the true fact is a quite different one, which cannot be easily guessed, but can certainly be proved. The fear of the anxiety-dream corresponds to a sex-feeling, a libidinous emotion, like every neurotic fear, and has, through the process of repression, proceeded from the libido.[9] In the interpretation of dreams, therefore, one must 174substitute for fear sexual excitement. The fear which has thus come into existence, exercises now—not regularly, but often—a selective influence on the dream-content and brings into the dream ideational elements which seem suitable to this fear for the conscious and erroneous conception of the dream. This is, as has been said, by no means regularly the case, for there are anxiety dreams in which the content is not at all frightful, in which, therefore, one cannot explain consciously the anxiety experienced.

I know that this explanation of fear in dreams sounds odd, and is not easily believed; but I can only advise making friends with it. It would, moreover, be remarkable if Norbert Hanold's dream allowed itself to be connected with this conception of fear and to be explained by it. We should then say that in the dreamer, at night, the erotic desire stirs, makes a powerful advance to bring his memory of the beloved into consciousness and thus snatch him from the delusion, experiences rejection and transformation into fear, which now, on its part, brings the fearful pictures from the academic memory of the dreamer into the dream-content. In this way the peculiar unconscious content of the dream, the amorous longing for the once known Zoë, is transformed into the manifest-content of the destruction of Pompeii and the loss of Gradiva.

I think that sounds quite plausible so far. One might justly demand that if erotic wishes form the undisfigured content of this dream, then one must be able to point out, in the transformed dream, at least a recognizable remnant of them hidden 175somewhere. Well, perhaps even this will come about with the help of a suggestion which appears later in the story. At the first meeting with the supposed Gradiva, Hanold remembers this dream and requests the apparition to lie down again as he has seen her.[10] Thereupon the young lady rises, indignant, and leaves her strange companion, in whose delusion-ridden speech she has heard the suggestion of an improper erotic wish. I think we may adopt Gradiva's interpretation; even from a real dream one cannot always demand more definiteness for the representation of an erotic wish.

Thus the application of some rules of dream-interpretation have been successful on Hanold's first dream, in making this dream comprehensible to us in its chief features, and in fitting it into the sequence of the story. Then it must probably have been produced by its author with due consideration for these rules. One could raise only one more question: why the author should introduce a dream for further development of the delusion. Well, I think that is very cleverly arranged and again keeps faith with reality. We have already heard that in actual illness the formation of a delusion is very often connected with a dream, but after our explanation of the nature of dreams, we need find no new riddle in this fact. Dreams and delusion spring from the same source, the repressed; the dream is, so to 176 speak, the physiological delusion of the normal human being. Before the repressed has become strong enough to push itself up into waking life as delusion, it may easily have won its first success under the more favourable circumstances of sleep, in the form of a dream having after-effects. During sleep, with the diminution of psychic activity, there enters a slackening in the strength of the resistance, which the dominant psychic forces oppose to the repressed. This slackening is what makes the dream-formation possible and therefore the dream becomes, for us, the best means of approach to knowledge of the unconscious psyche. Only the dream usually passes rapidly with the re-establishment of the psychic revival of waking life, and the ground won by the unconscious is again vacated.

177

III

In the further course of the story there is another dream, which can tempt us, even more perhaps than the first, to try to interpret it and fit it into the psychic life of the hero; but we save little if we leave the representation of the author of *Gradiva* here, to hasten directly to this second dream, for whoever wishes to interpret the dream of another, cannot help concerning himself, as extensively as possible, with every subjective and objective experience of the dreamer. Therefore it would be best to hold to the thread of the story and provide this with our commentaries as we progress.

The new delusion of the death of Gradiva at the destruction of Pompeii in the year 79 is not the only after-effect of the first dream analysed by us. Directly afterwards Hanold decides upon a trip to Italy, which finally takes him to Pompeii. Before this, however, something else has happened to him; leaning from his window, he thinks he sees on the street a figure with the bearing and walk of his Gradiva, hastens after her, in spite of his scanty attire, does not overtake her, but is driven back by the jeers of the people on the street. After he has returned to his room, the song of a canary whose cage hangs in the window of 178 the opposite house calls forth in him a mood such as if he wished to get from prison into freedom, and the spring trip is immediately decided upon and accomplished.

Our author has put this trip of Hanold's in an especially strong light, and has given to the latter partial clearness about his subjective processes. Hanold has, of course, given himself a scientific purpose for his journey, but this is not substantial. Yet he knows that the "impulse to travel has originated in a nameless feeling." A peculiar restlessness makes him dissatisfied with everything he encounters and drives him from Rome to Naples, from there to Pompeii, without his mood's being set right, even at the last halting-place. He is annoyed by the foolishness of honeymoon travellers, and is enraged over the boldness of house-flies, which populate the hotels of Pompeii; but finally he does not deceive himself over the fact that "his dissatisfaction was certainly not caused by his surroundings alone, but, to a degree, found its origin in him." He considers himself over-excited, feels "that he was out of sorts because he lacked something without being able to explain what, and this ill-humour he took everywhere with him." In such a mood he is enraged even at his mistress, science; as he wanders for the first time in the glow of the midday sun through Pompeii, all his science had left him without the least desire to rediscover it; "he remembered it as from a great distance, and he felt that it had been an old, dried-up, boresome aunt, dullest and most superfluous creature in the world." (*G.* p. 48.)

179 In this uncomfortable and confused state of mind, one of the riddles which are connected with this journey is solved for him at the moment when he first sees Gradiva walking through Pompeii; "he became conscious, for the first time, that he had, without himself knowing the motive in his heart, come to Italy on that account and had, without stop, continued from Rome and Naples to Pompeii to see if he could here find trace of her—and that in a literal sense—for, with her unusual gait, she must have left behind in the ashes a foot-print different from all the others." (*G.* p. 50.)

56

As our author has put so much care into the delineation of this trip, it must be worth our while to explain its relation to Hanold's delusion and its place in the sequence of events. The journey is undertaken for motives which the character does not at first recognize and does not admit until later, motives which our author designates directly as "unconscious." This is certainly true to life; one does not need to have a delusion to act thus; rather it is an everyday occurrence, even for normal people, that they are deceived about the motives of their actions and do not become conscious of them until subsequently, when a conflict of several emotional currents re-establishes for them the condition for such confusion. Hanold's trip, therefore, was intended, from the beginning, to serve the delusion, and was to take him to Pompeii to continue there the search for Gradiva. Let us remember that before, and directly after the dream, this search filled his mind and that the dream itself was only a stifled 180 answer of his consciousness to the question of the whereabouts of Gradiva. Some force which we do not recognize, however, next prevents the plan of the delusion from becoming conscious, so that only insufficient pretexts, which can be but partially revived, remain as a conscious motivation for the trip. The author gives us another riddle by having the dream, the discovery of the supposed Gradiva on the street, and the decision to make the journey because of the influence of the singing canary follow one another like chance occurrences without inner coherence.

With the help of the explanations which we gather from the later speeches of Zoë Bertgang, this obscure part of the tale is illuminated for our understanding. It was really the original of Gradiva, Miss Zoë, herself, whom Hanold saw from his window walking on the street (G. p. 23), and whom he would soon have overtaken. The statement of the dreamer— "she is really living now in the present, in the same city with you,"—would, therefore, by a lucky chance, have experienced an irrefutable corroboration, before which his inner resistance would have collapsed. The canary, however, whose song impelled Hanold to go away, belonged to Zoë, and his cage was in her window, in the house diagonally opposite from Hanold's (G. p. 98). Hanold, who, according to the girl's arraignment, was endowed with negative hallucination, understood the art of not seeing nor recognizing people, and must from the beginning have had unconscious knowledge of what we do not discover until later. The signs of Zoë's proximity, her appearance on the street, 181 and her bird's song so near his window intensify the effect of the dream, and in this condition, so dangerous for his resistance to the eroticism, he takes flight. The journey arises from the recovery of the resistance after that advance of erotic desire in the dream, an attempt at flight from the living and present beloved. It means practically a victory for repression, which, this time, in the delusion keeps the upper hand, as, in his former action, the "pedestrian investigations" of women and girls, the eroticism had been victorious. Everywhere, however, the indecision of the struggle, the compromise nature of the results was evident; the trip to Pompeii, which is to take him away from the living Zoë leads, at any rate, to her substitute, Gradiva. The journey, which is undertaken in defiance of the most recent dream-thoughts, follows, however, the order of the manifest dream-content to Pompeii. Thus delusion triumphs anew every time that eroticism and resistance struggle anew.

This conception of Hanold's trip, as a flight from the erotic desire for the beloved, who is so near, which is awakening in him, harmonizes, however, with the frame of mind portrayed in him during his stay in Italy. The rejection of the eroticism, which dominates him, expresses itself there in his abhorrence of honeymoon travellers. A little dream in the "albergo" in Rome, caused by the proximity of a couple of German lovers, "Augustus" and "Gretchen," whose evening conversation he is forced to overhear through the thin partition, casts a further light on the erotic tendencies of his first great dream. The new dream 182 transports him again to Pompeii where Vesuvius is just having another eruption, and thus refers to the dream which continues active during his trip; but among the imperilled people he sees this time—not as before himself and Gradiva—but Apollo Belvedere and the Capitoline Venus,—doubtless ironic exaltation of the couple in the adjoining room. Apollo lifts Venus, carries her away, and lays her on an object in the dark, which seems to be a carriage or a cart, for a "rattling sound" comes from it. Otherwise the dream needs no special skill for its interpretation. (G. p. 32.)

Our author, whom we have long relied on not to make a single stroke in his picture idly and without purpose, has given us another bit of testimony for the non-sexual force dominating Hanold on the trip. During hours of wandering in Pompeii, it happens that "remarkably, it did not once appear in his memory that he had dreamed some time ago that he had been present at the destruction of Pompeii by the volcanic eruption of 79." (G. p. 42.) At sight of Gradiva he first suddenly remembers this dream, and at the same time the motive of the delusion for his puzzling journey becomes conscious. Then what other meaning could there be for forgetting the dream, this repression-boundary between the dream and the psychic condition of the journey, than that the journey is not the result of the direct instigation of the dream, but of the rejection of this latter, as the emanation from a psychic force which desires no knowledge of the secret meaning of the dream?

183On the other hand, however, Hanold is not happy at this victory over his eroticism. The suppressed psychic impulse remains strong enough to revenge itself, by discontent and interception, on the suppressing agency. His longing has changed to restlessness and dissatisfaction, which make the trip seem senseless to him. His insight into the motivation of his trip is obstructed in service of the delusion; his relation to science, which ought, in such a place, to stir all his interest, is upset. So our author shows his hero, after flight from love, in a sort of crisis, in an utterly confused and unsettled condition, in a derangement such as usually appears at the climax of illness if neither of the two struggling forces is so much stronger than the other, that the difference could establish a strict, psychic régime. Here then our author takes hold to help and to settle, for, at this place, he introduces Gradiva, who undertakes the cure of the delusion. With his power to direct to a happy solution the fortunes of all the characters created by him, in spite of all the requirements which he has them conform to, he transports the girl, from whom Hanold has fled to Pompeii, to that very place and thus corrects the folly which the delusion caused the young man to commit in leaving the home-city of his beloved for the dead abode of the one substituted for her by his fancy.

With the appearance of Zoë Bertgang as Gradiva, which marks the climax of the suspense of the story, our interest is soon diverted. If we have hitherto been living through the developments of a delusion, we shall now become witnesses 184of its cure, and may ask ourselves if our author has merely invented the procedure of this cure or has carried it out according to actually existing possibilities. From Zoë's own words in the conversation with her friend, we have decidedly the right to ascribe to her the intention to cure the hero (G. p. 97). But how does she go about it? After she has cast aside the indignation which the unreasonable request, to lie down to sleep again, as "then," had evoked in her, she appears again next day, at the same place, and elicits from Hanold all the secret knowledge that was lacking to her for an understanding of his conduct of the previous day. She learns of his dream, of the bas-relief of Gradiva, and of the peculiarity of walk which she shares with the relief. She accepts the rôle of a spirit awakened to life for a short hour, which, she observes, his delusion assigns to her, and in ambiguous words, she gently puts him in the way of a new rôle by accepting from him the grave-flower which he had brought along without conscious purpose, and expresses regret that he has not given her roses (G. p. 70).

Our interest in the conduct of the eminently clever girl, who has decided to win the lover of her youth as husband, after she has recognized his love behind his delusion as its impelling force, is, however, restrained at this place probably because of the strange feelings that the delusion can arouse even in us. Its latest development, that Gradiva, who was buried in the year 79, can now exchange conversation with him as a noon-spirit, for an hour, after the passing of which she 185sinks out of sight or seeks her grave again, this chimæra, which is not confused by the perception of her modern foot-covering, nor by her ignorance of the ancient tongues, nor by her command of German, which did not exist in former times, seems indeed to justify the author's designation, "A Pompeiian Fancy," but to exclude every standard of clinical reality; and yet on closer consideration the improbability in this delusion seems to me, for the most part, to vanish. To be sure, our author has taken upon himself a part of the blame, and in the first part of the story has offered the fact that Zoë was the image of the bas-relief in every trait. One must, therefore, guard against transferring the improbability of this preliminary to its logical conclusion that Hanold considers the girl to be

Gradiva come to life. The explanation of the delusion is here enhanced by the fact that our author has offered us no rational disposal of it. In the glowing sun of the Campagna and in the bewildering magic powers of the vine which grows on Vesuvius, our author has introduced helpful and mitigating circumstances of the transgression of the hero. The most important of all explanatory and exonerating considerations remains, however, the facility with which our intellect decides to accept an absurd content if impulses with a strong emotional stress find thereby their satisfaction. It is astonishing, and generally meets with too little acceptance, how easily and often intelligent people, under such psychological constellations, give the reactions of partial mental weakness, and any one who is not too conceited may observe this in himself as often 186as he wishes, and especially when a part of the thought-processes under consideration is connected with unconscious or repressed motives. I cite, in this connection, the words of a philosopher who writes to me, "I have also begun to make note of cases of striking mistakes, from my own experience, and of thoughtless actions which one subsequently explains to himself (in a very unreasonable way). It is amazing but typical how much stupidity thereby comes to light." Now let us consider the fact that belief in spirits, apparitions and returning souls (which finds so much support in the religions to which, at least as children, we have all clung) is by no means destroyed among all educated people, and that many otherwise reasonable people find their interest in spiritism compatible with their reason. Yes, even one become dispassionate and incredulous may perceive with shame how easily he turns back for a moment to a belief in spirits, when emotions and perplexity concur in him. I know of a physician who had once lost a patient by Basedow's disease and could not rid himself of the slight suspicion that he had perhaps contributed by unwise medication to the unfortunate outcome. One day several years later there stepped into his office a girl, in whom, in spite of all reluctance, he was obliged to recognize the dead woman. His only thought was that it was true that the dead could return, and his fear did not give way to shame until the visitor introduced herself as the sister of the woman who had died of that disease. Basedow's disease lends to those afflicted with it a great similarity of features, which has often been noticed, and in this case 187the typical resemblance was far more exaggerated than the family resemblance. The physician, moreover, to whom this happened was I, and therefore I am not inclined to quarrel with Norbert Hanold over the clinical possibility of his short delusion about Gradiva, who had returned to life. That in serious cases of chronic delusion (paranoia) the most extreme absurdities, ingeniously devised and well supported, are active is, finally, well known to every psychiatrist.

After his first meeting with Gradiva, Norbert Hanold had drunk his wine in first one and then another of the hotels of Pompeii known to him, while the other guests were having their regular meals. "Of course, in no way had the absurd supposition entered his mind" that he was doing this to find out what hotel Gradiva lived and ate in, but it is hard to say what other significance his action could have. On the day after his second meeting in Meleager's house, he has all sorts of remarkable and apparently disconnected experiences; he finds a narrow cleft in the wall of the portico where Gradiva had disappeared, meets a foolish lizard-catcher, who addresses him as an acquaintance, discovers a secluded hotel, the "Albergo del Sole," whose owner talks him into buying a metal brooch encrusted with green patina, which had been found with the remains of a Pompeiian girl, and finally notices in his own hotel a newly-arrived young couple, whom he diagnoses to be brother and sister, and congenial. All these impressions are then woven into a "remarkably nonsensical" dream as follows:

"Somewhere in the sun Gradiva sat making a 188trap out of a blade of grass in order to catch a lizard, and she said, 'Please stay quite still—my colleague is right; the method is really good and she has used it with the greatest success.'"

To this dream he offers resistance even while sleeping, with the critique that it is indeed the most utter madness, and he casts about to free himself from it. He succeeds in doing this, too, with the aid of an invisible bird who utters a short, merry call, and carries the lizard away in his beak.

Shall we risk an attempt to interpret this dream also, that is, to substitute for it the latent thoughts from whose disfigurement it must have proceeded? It is as nonsensical as one could expect a dream to be and this absurdity of dreams is the mainstay of the view which denies to the dream the character of a valid psychic act, and has it proceed from a desultory stimulus of the psychic elements.

We can apply to this dream the technique which can be designated as the regular procedure of dream-interpretation. It consists in disregarding the apparent sequence in the manifest dream but in examining separately every part of the content, and in seeking its derivation in the impressions, memories and free ideas of the dreamer. As we cannot examine Hanold, however, we must be satisfied with reference to his impressions, and may with due caution substitute our own ideas for his.

"Somewhere in the sun Gradiva sat catching lizards, and said ..." What impression of the day is this part of the dream reminiscent of? [189]Unquestionably of the meeting with the older man, the lizard-catcher, for whom Gradiva is substituted in the dream. He was sitting or lying on a "hot, sunny" slope and spoke to Hanold, too. Even the utterances of Gradiva in the dream are copied from those of the man. Let us compare: "'The method suggested by my colleague, Eimer, is really good; I have already used it often with the best of success. Please remain quite still.'"—Quite similarly Gradiva speaks in the dream, only that for the *colleague, Eimer,* is substituted an unnamed woman-colleague; the *often* from the zoologist's speech is missing in the dream, and the connection between the statements has been somewhat changed. It seems, therefore, that this experience of the day has been transformed into a dream by some changes and disfigurements. Why thus, and what is the meaning of the disfigurements, the substitution of Gradiva for the old gentleman, and the introduction of the puzzling "woman-colleague"?

There is a rule of dream-interpretation as follows: A speech heard in a dream always originates from a speech either heard or uttered in waking life. Well, this rule seems followed here; the speech of Gradiva is only a modification of a speech heard in the daytime from the zoologist. Another rule of dream-interpretation would tell us that the substitution of one person for another, or the mixture of two people by showing one in a position which characterizes the other means equivalence of the two people, a correspondence between them. Let us venture to apply this rule also to our dream; then the interpretation would follow: "Gradiva [190]catches lizards, as that old gentleman does, and like him, is skilled in lizard-catching." This result is not comprehensible yet, but we have another riddle before us. To which impression of the day shall we refer the "woman colleague," who is substituted in the dream for the famous zoologist, Eimer? We have here fortunately not much choice; only one other girl can be meant by "woman-colleague," the congenial young lady in whom Hanold has conjectured a sister travelling with her brother. "In her gown she wore a red Sorrento rose, the sight of which, as he looked across from his corner, stirred something in his memory without his being able to think what it was." This observation on the part of the author surely gives us the right to assert that she is the "woman-colleague" of the dream. What Hanold cannot remember is certainly nothing but the remark of the supposed Gradiva, as she asked him for the grave-flower, that to more fortunate girls one brought roses in spring. In this speech, however, lay a hidden wooing. What kind of lizard-catching is it that this more fortunate woman-colleague has been so successful with?

On the next day Hanold surprises the supposed brother and sister in tender embrace and can thus correct his mistake of the previous day. They are really a couple of lovers, on their honeymoon, as we later learn, when the two disturb, so unexpectedly, Hanold's third meeting with Zoë. If we will now accept the idea that Hanold, who consciously considers them brother and sister, has, in his unconscious, recognized at once their [191]real relation, which on the next day betrays itself so unequivocally, there results a good meaning for Gradiva's remark in the dream. The red rose then becomes a symbol for being in love; Hanold understands that the two are as Gradiva and he are soon to be; the lizard-catching acquires the meaning of husband-catching, and Gradiva's speech means something like this: "Let me arrange things; I know how to win a husband as well as this other girl does."

Why must this penetration of Zoë's intentions appear throughout in the form of the speech of the old zoologist? Why is Zoë's skill in husband-catching represented by that of the old man in lizard-catching? Well, it is easy for us to answer that question; we have long ago guessed that the lizard-catcher is none other than the professor of zoology, Bertgang, Zoë's father, who must, of course, also know Hanold, so that it is a matter of course that he addresses Hanold as an acquaintance. Again, let us accept the idea that Hanold, in his unconscious, immediately recognizes the professor—"It seemed to him dimly that he had already seen the face of the lizard-hunter probably in one of the two hotels." Thus is explained the strange cloaking of the purpose attributed to Zoë. She is the daughter of the lizard-catcher; she has inherited this skill from him. The substitution of Gradiva for the lizard-catcher in the dream-content, is, therefore, the representation of the relation between the two people, which was recognized by the unconscious; the introduction of "woman-colleague" in place of *colleague, Eimer,* allows the dream to express comprehension of her courtship of the man. The dream has welded two of the day's experiences in one situation, "condensed" as we say, in order to procure, to be sure, very indiscernible expression for two ideas which are not allowed to become conscious; but we can go on diminishing the strangeness of the dream still more and pointing out the influence of other experiences of the day on the formation of the manifest dream.

Dissatisfied by the former information, we might explain why the scene of the lizard-catching was made the nucleus of the dream, and suppose that the other elements in the dream-thoughts influence the term "lizard" in the manifest dream. It might really be very easy. Let us recall that Hanold has discovered a cleft in the wall, in the place where Gradiva seems to him to disappear; this is "wide enough to afford passage to an unusually slender figure." By this perception he is forced in the day-time to an alteration in his delusion; Gradiva did not sink into the ground when she disappeared from his sight, but was going back, by this route, to her grave. In his unconscious thought he might say to himself that he had now found the natural explanation for the surprising disappearance of the girl; but must not forcing one's self through narrow clefts, and disappearing in such clefts recall the conduct of lizards? Does not Gradiva herself, then, in this connection, behave like an agile little lizard? We think, therefore, that the discovery of this cleft in the wall had worked as a determinant on the choice of the "lizard" element for the manifest dream-content; the lizard-situation of the dream, therefore, represented this impression of the day, and the meeting with the zoologist, Zoë's father.

What if, become bold, we now wished to attempt to find in the dream-content a representation also for the one experience of the day which has not yet been turned to account, the discovery of the third hotel, "del Sole"? Our author has treated this episode so exhaustively and linked so much with it, we should be surprised if it, alone, had yielded no contribution to the dream-formation. Hanold enters this hotel, which, because of its secluded situation and its distance from the station, has remained unknown to him, to get a bottle of lime-water for congestion of blood. The hotel-keeper uses this opportunity to extol his antiques and shows him a brooch which, it was alleged, had belonged to that Pompeiian girl who was found near the Forum in fond embrace with her lover. Hanold, who had never before believed this frequently repeated story, is now compelled, by a force strange to him, to believe in the truth of this touching story and in the genuineness of the article found, buys the brooch and leaves the hotel with his purchase. In passing, he sees nodding down at him from one of the windows a cluster of white, asphodel blossoms which had been placed in a water-glass, and he feels that this sight is an attestation of the genuineness of his new possession. The sincere conviction is now impressed upon him that the green brooch belonged to Gradiva, and that she was the girl who died in her lover's embrace. The tormenting jealousy, which thereupon seizes him, he appeases with the resolution to assure himself about this suspicion, the next day, from Gradiva, herself, by showing the brooch. This is a strange bit of new delusion; and shouldn't any trace point to it in the dream of the following night?

It will be well worth our while to get an understanding of the origin of this augmentation of the delusion, to look up the new unconscious idea for which the new bit of delusion is substituted. The delusion originates under the influence of the proprietor of the "Sun Hotel," toward whom Hanold conducts himself in so remarkably credulous a manner, as if he has received a suggestion from him. The proprietor shows him a small metal brooch as genuine, and as the possession of that girl who was found in the arms of her lover, buried in the ashes, and Hanold, who could be critical enough to doubt the truth of the story as well as the genuineness of the brooch, is caught, credulous, and buys the more than doubtful antique. It is quite incomprehensible why he should act so, and no hint is given that the personality of the proprietor himself might solve this riddle for us. There is, however, another riddle in this incident, and two riddles sometimes solve each other. On leaving the "albergo," he catches sight of an asphodel cluster in a glass at a window, and finds in it an attestation of the genuineness of the metal brooch. How can that be? This last stroke is fortunately easy of solution. The white flower is, of course, the one which he presented to Gradiva at noon, and it is quite right that through the sight of it at one of the windows of this hotel, something is corroborated, not the genuineness of the brooch, but 195something else which has become clear to him at the discovery of this formerly overlooked "albergo." In the forenoon he has already acted as if he were seeking, in the two hotels of Pompeii, where the person lived who appeared to him as Gradiva. Now, as he stumbles so unexpectedly upon a third, he must say in the unconscious: "So she lives here"; and then, on leaving: "Right there is the asphodel flower I gave her; that is, therefore, her window." This, then, is the new idea for which the delusion is substituted, and which cannot become conscious because its assumption that Gradiva is living, a person known by him, cannot become conscious.

How then is the substitution of the delusion for the new idea supposed to have occurred? I think thus: that the feeling of conviction which clung to the idea was able to assert itself and persisted, while another ideational content related to it by thought-connection acted as substitute for the idea itself which was incapable of consciousness. Thus the feeling of conviction was connected with a really strange content, and this latter attained, as delusion, a recognition which did not belong to it. Hanold transfers his conviction that Gradiva lives in this house to other impressions which he receives in this house, becomes, in a way, credulous about what the proprietor says, the genuineness of the metal brooch, and the truth of the anecdote about the lovers found in an embrace, but only by this route, that he connects what he has heard in this house with Gradiva. The jealousy which has been lying ready in him gets possession of this material, and even in contradiction to his first 196dream there appears the delusion that Gradiva was the girl who died in the arms of her lover, and that the brooch which he bought belonged to her.

We notice that the conversation with Gradiva, and her gentle wooing "through the flower," have already evoked important changes in Hanold. Traits of male desire, components of the libido are awakened in him, which, to be sure, cannot yet dispense with the concealment through conscious pretexts; but the problem of the corporeal nature of Gradiva, which has pursued him this whole day, cannot disavow its derivation from the erotic desire of the young man for possession of the woman, even if it is dragged into the scientific world by conscious stress on Gradiva's peculiar hovering between life and death. Jealousy is an added mark of Hanold's awakening activity in love; he expresses this at the opening of the conversation on the next day, and with the aid of a new pretext achieves his object of touching the girl's body, and of striking her, as in times long past.

Now, however, it is time to ask if the course of delusion-formation which we have inferred from our author's representation is one otherwise admitted or possible. From my experience as physician, I can answer only that it is surely the right way, perhaps the only one, in which the delusion receives the unswerving recognition due to its clinical character. If the patient believes in his delusion so firmly, it does not happen because of inversion of his powers of judgment, and does not proceed from what is erroneous in the 197delusion; but in every delusion there lies also a little grain of truth; there is something in it which really deserves belief, and this is the source of the conviction of the patient, who is, to this extent, justified. This true element, however, has been repressed for a long time; if it finally succeeds in pushing into consciousness (this time in disfigured form), the feeling of a conviction clinging to it, as if in compensation, is over-strong and now clings to and protects the disfigurement-substitute of the repressed, true element against every critical impugnment. The conviction at once shifts itself from the unconscious, true element to the conscious, erroneous one connected with it, and remains fixed there as a result of this very displacement. The case of delusion-formation which resulted from Hanold's first dream is nothing but a similar, if not identical, case of such displacement. Yes, the depicted manner of development of conviction in the delusion is not fundamentally different from the way in which conviction is formed in normal cases, where repression does not enter into play. All our convictions lie in thought-contents in which the true and the false are combined and *they stretch over the former and the latter.* They differentiate at once between the true and whatever false is associated with it and protect this, even if not so immutably as in the delusion, against merited critique. Associations, protection, likewise, have their own value even for normal psychology.

I will now return to the dream and lay stress on a small, but not uninteresting feature which establishes a connection between two occasions of the 198dream. Gradiva had placed the white asphodel flower in definite contrast to the red rose; the finding of the asphodel flower again in the window of the "Albergo del Sole" becomes a weighty proof for Hanold's unconscious idea which expresses itself in a new delusion; and to this is added the fact that the red rose in the dress of the congenial young girl helps Hanold again, in the unconscious, to a right estimation of her relation to her companion so that he can have her enter the dream as "woman colleague."

But where in the manifest dream-content is found the trace and representation of that discovery of Hanold's for which we find that the new delusion is substituted, the discovery that Gradiva lives with her father in the third hotel of Pompeii, the "Albergo del Sole," which he has not been acquainted with? Well, it stands in its entirety and not even much disfigured in the dream; but I dread to point it out, for I know that even with the readers whose patience with me has lasted so long, a strong opposition to my attempts at interpretation will be stirred up. Hanold's discovery is given in full in the dream-content, I repeat, but so cleverly concealed that one must needs overlook it. It is hidden there behind a play on words, an ambiguity. "Somewhere in the sun Gradiva sat"; this we have rightly connected with the locality where Hanold met the zoologist, her father; but can it not also mean in the "Sun," that is, in the "Albergo del Sole," in the "Sun Hotel" Gradiva lives? And doesn't the "somewhere" which has no reference to the meeting with her father sound so 199hypocritically indefinite for the very reason that it introduces the definite information about the whereabouts of Gradiva? According to previous experience in the interpretation of real dreams, I am quite sure of such a meaning in the ambiguity, but I should really not venture to offer this bit of interpretation to my readers, if our author did not lend me here his powerful assistance. On the next day he puts into the mouth of the girl, when she sees the metal brooch, the same pun which we accept for the interpretation of the dream-content. "Did you find it in the sun, perhaps? It brings to light many such works of art"; and as Hanold does not understand the speech, she explains that she means the "Sun Hotel," which is called "Sole" here, whence the supposed antique is also familiar to her.

And now may we make the attempt to substitute for Hanold's "remarkably nonsensical" dream unconscious thoughts hidden behind it and as unlike it as possible? It runs somewhat as follows: "She lives in the 'Sun' with her father; why is she playing such a game with me? Does she wish to make fun of me? Or could it be possible that she loves me and wishes me for a husband?" To this latter possibility there now follows in sleep the rejection, "That is the most utter madness," which is apparently directed against the whole manifest dream.

Critical readers have now the right to inquire about the origin of that interpolation, not formerly established, which refers to being made fun of by Gradiva. To this *Traumdeutung* gives the answer; if in dream-thoughts, taunts and 200sneers, or bitter contradictions occur, they are expressed by the nonsensical course of the manifest dream, through the absurdity in the dream. The latter means, therefore, no paralysis of psychic activity, but is one of the means of representation which the dream-work makes use of. As always in especially difficult passages, our author here comes to our assistance. The nonsensical dream has another postlude in which a bird utters a merry call and takes away the lizard in his beak. Such a laughing call Hanold had heard after Gradiva's disappearance. It really came from Zoë who was shaking off the melancholy seriousness of her lower world rôle; with this laugh Gradiva had really derided him. The dream-picture, however, of the bird carrying away the lizard may recall that other one in a former dream in which Apollo Belvedere carried away the Capitoline Venus.

Perhaps the impression now exists with many readers that the interpretation of the lizard-catching situation by the idea of wooing is not sufficiently justified. Additional support is found here, perhaps in the hint that Zoë, in conversation with her colleague, admits about herself that very thing which Hanold's thoughts suppose about her, when she tells that she had been sure of "digging up" something interesting for herself here in Pompeii. She thereby delves into the archæological series of associations as he did into the zoological with his allegory of lizard-catching, as if they were opposing each other and each wished to assume properties of the other.

201Thus we have finished the interpretation of the second dream. Both have become accessible to our understanding under the presupposition that the dreamer, in his unconscious thought, knows all that he has, he has in the former rightly judged everything which, in the latter, he delusively misconstrues. In this connection we have, of course, been obliged to make many assertions which sounded odd to the reader because they were strange to him and probably often awakened the suspicion that we were giving out as our author's meaning what is only our own meaning. We are ready to do everything to dissipate this suspicion and will therefore gladly consider more exhaustively one of the most knotty points—I mean the use of ambiguous words and speeches as in the example, "Somewhere in the Sun Gradiva sat."

It must be striking to every reader of *Gradiva* how often our author puts into the mouths of both the leading characters speeches which have double meaning. For Hanold these speeches are intended to have only one meaning, and only his companion, Gradiva, is affected by their other meaning. Thus, after her first answer, he exclaims: "I knew that your voice sounded so," and the yet unenlightened Zoë has to ask how that is possible, as he has never before heard her speak. In the second conversation, the girl is for a moment puzzled by his delusion, as he assures her that he recognized her at once. She must understand these words in the meaning that is correct for his unconscious, as his recognition of their acquaintance which reaches back into 202childhood, while he, of course, knows nothing of this meaning of his speech and explains it only by reference to the delusion which dominates him. The speeches of the girl, on the other hand, in whose person the most brilliant mental clarity is opposed to the delusion, are made intentionally ambiguous. One meaning of them falls in with the ideas of Hanold's delusion, in order to enable her to penetrate into his conscious comprehension, the other raises itself above the delusion, and, as a rule, gives us the interpretation of it in the unconscious truth which has been represented by it. It is a triumph of wit to be able to represent the delusion and the truth in the same expression.

Interspersed with such ambiguities is Zoë's speech in which she explains the situation to her girl friend and at the same time rids herself of her disturbing society; it is really spoken out of the book, calculated more for us readers than for her happy colleague. In the conversations with Hanold, the double meaning is chiefly established by the fact that Zoë makes use of the symbolism which we find followed in Hanold's first dream, in the equivalence of repression and destruction, Pompeii and childhood. Thus on the one hand she can, in her speeches, continue in the rôle which Hanold's delusion assigns to her, on the other, she can touch upon the real relations, and awaken in Hanold's unconscious a knowledge of them.

"I have long accustomed myself to being dead." (*G.* p. 70.) "For me, the flower of oblivion is the right one from your hand" (*G.* 203p. 70). In these speeches is given lightly the reproof which then breaks out clearly enough in her last sermon when she compares him to an archæopteryx. "That a person must die to become alive again; but for archæologists that is, of course, necessary" (*G.* p. 102), she continues after the solution of the delusion as if to give us the key to her ambiguous speeches. The most beautiful symbolism appears, however, in the question (*G.* p. 88): "It seems to me as if we had already eaten our bread thus together once two thousand years ago. Can't you remember it?" In this speech the substitution of historic antiquity for childhood, and the effort to awaken his memory of the latter are quite unmistakable.

Whence, therefore, comes this striking preference for ambiguous speeches in *Gradiva*? It seems to us not chance, but the necessary sequence from the preliminaries of the tale. It is nothing but the counterpart of the twofold determination of symptoms in so far as the

64

speeches are themselves symptoms and proceed from compromises between the conscious and the unconscious; but one notices this double origin in the speeches more easily than in the acts; and when, as the pliability of the material of conversation often makes possible, each of the two intentions of a speech succeeds by the same arrangement of words in expressing itself well, then there is present what we call an "ambiguity."

During the psychotherapeutic treatment of a delusion, or an analogous disturbance, one often evolves such ambiguous speeches in patients as 204new symptoms of the most fleeting duration, and can even succeed in making use of them, whereby, with the meaning intended for the consciousness of the patient, one can, not infrequently, stimulate the understanding for the one valid in the unconscious. I know from experience that among the uninitiate this rôle of ambiguity usually gives the greatest offence, and causes the grossest misunderstanding, but our author was right, at any rate, in representing in his production this characteristic feature of the processes of the formation of dream and delusion.

205

IV

With Zoë's entrance as physician there is awakened in us, we said, a new interest. We are eager to learn if such a cure as she accomplishes on Hanold is comprehensible or possible, whether our author has observed the conditions of the passing of a delusion as correctly as those of its development.

Without doubt a view will be advanced denying to the case portrayed by our author such a principal interest, and recognizing no problem requiring an explanation. For Hanold nothing more remains, it might be asserted, but to solve his delusion again, after its object, the supposed Gradiva, conveys to him the incorrectness of all his assertions and gives him the most natural explanations for everything puzzling; for example, how she knows his name. Thereby the affair would be settled logically; as, however, the girl in this case has confessed her love, for the satisfaction of his feminine readers, our author would surely allow the otherwise not uninteresting story to end in the usually happy way, marriage. More consistent, and just as possible, would have been the different conclusion that the young scholar, after the explanation of his mistake, should, with polite thanks, take his leave of the young lady and in that way 206motivate the rejection of her love so that he might offer an intense interest to ancient women of bronze or stone, or the originals of these, if they were attainable, but might have no idea of how to deal with a girl of flesh and blood of his own time. The archæological fancy was most arbitrarily cemented into a love-story by our author, himself.

In discountenancing this conception as impossible, our attention is first called to the fact that we have to attribute the change beginning in Norbert Hanold not to the relinquishment of the delusion alone. At the same time, indeed before the solution of the latter, there is in him an undeniable awakening of the desire for love, which, of course, results in his asking for the hand of the girl who has freed him from delusion. We have already shown under what pretexts and cloakings, curiosity about her corporeal nature, jealousy, and the brutal male impulse for possession are expressed in him in the midst of the delusion, since repressed desire put the first dream into his mind. Let us add the further testimony that in the evening after the second talk with Gradiva a living woman for the first time seems congenial to him, although he still makes the concession to his abhorrence of honeymoon travellers, by not recognizing the congenial girl as newly married. The next forenoon, however, chance makes him witness of an exchange of caresses between the girl and her supposed brother, and he draws back shyly as if he had disturbed a holy ceremony. Disdain for "Augustus" and "Gretchen" is forgotten and respect for love is restored to him.

Thus our author has connected the treatment 207of the delusion and the breaking forth of the desire for love most closely with one another, and prepared the outcome in a love-affair as necessary. He knows the nature of the delusion even better than his critics; he knows that a component of amorous desire has combined with a component of resistance in the formation of the delusion, and he has the girl who undertakes the cure discover in Hanold's delusion the component referring to her. Only this insight can make her decide to devote herself to treating him, only the certainty of knowing herself loved by him can move her to confess to him her love. The treatment consists in restoring to him, from without, the

65

repressed memories which he cannot release from within; it would be ineffective if the therapeutist did not consider the emotions; and the interpretation of the delusion would not finally be: "See; all that means only that you love me."

The procedure which our author has his Zoë follow for the cure of the delusion of the friend of her youth, shows a considerable resemblance, no, complete agreement, essentially, with a therapeutic method which Dr. J. Breuer and the present writer introduced into medicine in 1895, and to the perfection of which the latter has since devoted himself. This method of treatment, first called the "cathartic" by Breuer, which the present writer has preferred to designate as "analytic," consists in rather forcibly bringing into the consciousness of the patients who suffer from disturbances analogous to Hanold's delusion, the unconscious, through the repression of which they have become ill, just as Gradiva does with the 208repressed memories of their childhood relations. To be sure, accomplishment of this task is easier for Gradiva than for the physician; she is, in this connection, in a position which might be called ideal from many view-points. The physician who does not fathom his patient in advance, and does not possess within himself, as conscious memory, what is working in the patient as unconscious, must call to his aid a complicated technique in order to overcome this disadvantage. He must learn to gather with absolute certainty, from the patient's conscious ideas and statements, the repressed material in him, to guess the unconscious, when it betrays itself behind the patient's conscious expressions and acts. The latter then does something similar to what Norbert Hanold did at the end of the story, when he re-translates the name, Gradiva, into *Bertgang*. The disturbance disappears then by being traced back to its origin; analysis brings cure at the same time.

The similarity between the procedure of Gradiva and the analytic method of psychotherapy is, however, not limited to these two points, making the repressed conscious, and the concurrence of explanation and cure. It extends itself to what proves the essential of the whole change, the awakening of the emotions. Every disturbance analogous to Hanold's delusion, which in science we usually designate as a psychoneurosis, has, as a preliminary, the repression of part of the emotional life, to speak boldly, of the sex-impulse, and at every attempt to introduce the unconscious and repressed cause of illness into consciousness, the emotional component necessarily awakens to 209renewed struggle with the forces repressing it, to adjust itself for final result, often under violent manifestations of reaction. In reawakening, in consciousness, of repressed love, the process of recuperation is accomplished when we sum up all the various components of sex-impulse as "love," and this reawakening is irremissible, for the symptoms on account of which the treatment was undertaken are nothing but the precipitations of former struggles of repression and recurrence and can be solved and washed away only by a new high-tide of these very passions. Every psychoanalytic treatment is an attempt to free repressed love, which has formed a miserable compromise-outlet in a symptom. Yes, the conformity with the therapeutic process pictured by the author in *Gradiva* reaches its height when we add that even in analytical psychotherapy the reawakened passion, whether love or hate, chooses the person of the physician as its object every time.

Then, of course, appear the differences which make the case of Gradiva an ideal one such as the technique of physicians cannot attain. Gradiva can respond to the love which is pushing through from the unconscious into the conscious; the physician cannot; Gradiva was herself the object of the former repressed love; her person offers at once a desirable object to the freed erotic activity. The physician has been a stranger, and after the cure must try to become a stranger again; often he does not know how to advise the cured patient to apply in life her regained capacity for love. To suggest what resources and makeshifts the physician then employs to approach with more or 210less success the model of a love-cure which our author has drawn for us, would carry us too far away from our present task.

Now, however, the last question which we have already evaded answering several times. Our views about repression, the formation of delusion and related disturbances, the formation and interpretation of dreams, the rôle of erotic life, and the manner of cure for such disturbances are, of course, not by any means the common property of science, to say nothing of being the possession of educated people. If the insight which makes our author able to create his "Fancy" in such a way that we can analyse it like a real history of disease has for its foundation the above-mentioned knowledge, we should like to find out the source of it. One of the circle who, as was explained at the beginning, was interested in the dreams of *Gradiva* and their possible interpretation, put the direct question to Wilhelm Jensen, whether any such similar theories of science had been known to him. Our author answered, as was to be expected, in the negative, and rather testily. His imagination had put into his mind the *Gradiva* in whom he had his joy; any one whom she did not please might leave her alone. He did not suspect how much she had pleased the readers.

It is easily possible that our author's rejection does not stop at that. Perhaps he denies knowledge of the rules which we have shown that he follows, and disavows all the intentions which we recognized in his production; I do not consider this improbable; then, however, only two possibilities remain. Either we have presented a true 211caricature of interpretation, by transferring to a harmless work of art tendencies of which its creator had no idea, and have thereby shown again how easy it is to find what one seeks and what one is engrossed with, a possibility of which most strange examples are recorded in the history of literature. Every reader may now decide for himself whether he cares to accept such an explanation; we, of course, hold fast to the other, still remaining view. We think that our author needed to know nothing of such rules and intentions, so that he may disavow them in good faith, and that we have surely found nothing in his romance which was not contained in it. We are probably drawing from the same source, working over the same material, each of us with a different method, and agreement in results seems to vouch for the fact that both have worked correctly. Our procedure consists of the conscious observation of abnormal psychic processes in others, in order to be able to discover and express their laws. Our author proceeds in another way; he directs his attention to the unconscious in his own psyche, listens to its possibilities of development and grants them artistic expression, instead of suppressing them with conscious critique. Thus he learns from himself what we learn from others, what laws the activity of this unconscious must follow, but he does not need to express these laws, need not even recognize them clearly; they are, as a result of his intelligent patience, contained incarnate in his creatures. We unfold these laws by analysis of his fiction as we discover them from cases of real illness, but the conclusion seems 212irrefutable, that either both (our author, as well as the physician) have misunderstood the unconscious in the same way or we have both understood it correctly. This conclusion is very valuable for us; for its sake, it was worth while for us to investigate the representation of the formation and cure of delusion, as well as the dreams, in Jensen's *Gradiva* by the methods of therapeutic psychoanalysis.

We have reached the end. An observant reader might remind us that, at the beginning, we had remarked that dreams are wishes represented as fulfilled and that we still owe the proof of it. Well, we reply, our arguments might well show how unjustifiable it would be to wish to cover the explanations which we have to give of the dream with the formula that the dream is a wish-fulfilment; but the assertion stands, and is also easy to demonstrate for the dreams in *Gradiva*. The latent dream-thoughts—we know now what is meant by that—may be of numerous kinds; in *Gradiva* they are day-remnants, thoughts which are left over unheard, and not disposed of by the psychic activity of waking life. In order that a dream may originate from them the co-operation of a—generally unconscious— wish is required; this establishes the motive power for the dream-formation; the day-remnants give the material for it. In Norbert Hanold's first dream two wishes concur in producing the dream, one capable of consciousness, the other, of course, belonging to the unconscious, and active because of repression. This was the wish, comprehensible to every archæologist, to have been an eye-witness of that 213catastrophe of 79. What sacrifice would be too great, for an antiquarian, to realize this wish otherwise than through dreams! The other wish and dream-maker is of an erotic nature: to be present when the beloved lies down to sleep, to express it crudely. It is the rejection of this which makes the dream an anxiety-dream. Less striking are, perhaps, the impelling wishes of the second dream, but if we recall its interpretation, we shall not hesitate to pronounce it also erotic. The wish to be captured by the beloved, to yield and surrender to her, as it may be construed behind the lizard-catching, has really a passive masochistic character. On the next day the dreamer strikes the beloved, as if under the sway of the antagonistic, erotic force; but we must stop or we may forget that Hanold and Gradiva are only creatures of our author.

THE END

Printed in Great Britain by
UNWIN BROTHERS, LIMITED, THE GRESHAM PRESS, WOXING AND LONDON

[Footnotes]

1] Freud, *Traumdeutung*, 1900 (Leipzig and Wien, 1911), translated by A. A. Brill, M.D., Ph.B. *Interpretation of Dreams*, George Allen and Unwin, Ltd., 1913.

2] The case N.H. would have to be designated as hysterical, not paranoiac delusion. The marks of paranoia are lacking here.

3] See the important work by E. Bleuler, Affektivität, Suggestibilität, Paranoia, translated by Dr. Charles Ricksher in N. Y. State Hospitals Bulletin, Feb., 1912, and *Die diagnostischen Assoziationsstudien* by C. Jung, both Zürich, 1906.

4] Cf. Freud: *Sammlung der kleiner Schriften zur Neurosenlehre*, 1906. Translated in part by A. A. Brill, M.D., Ph.B. Nervous and Mental Diseases Monograph Series No. 4. Selected Papers on Hysteria and other Psychoneuroses. N. Y., 1912.

5] Cf. *Bruchstück einer Hysterie-Analyse*, 1905.

6] Cf. Breuer u. Freud, *Studien, über Hysterie*, 1905. Leipzig and Wien, translated by A. A. Brill, M.D., Ph.B. Nervous and Mental Diseases Monograph Series No. 4. Selected Papers on Hysteria and other Psychoneuroses.

7] *Sante de Sanctis*, I. Sogni. (Original in Italian.) Translated into German, *Die Träume*, by Mr. Otto Schmidt, 1901, Hallé, a. S.

8] Compare the text of *Gradiva*, p. 21.

9] Cf. *Sammlung kl. Schriften zur Neurosenlehre*, V., and *Traumdeutung*, p. 344. *Traumdeutung* translated by A. A. Brill, M.D., Ph.B., *Interpretation of Dreams*, George Allen and Unwin, Ltd., 1913 (p. 441).

10] G. p. 57: "No—not talked—but I called to you when you lay down to sleep and stood near you then—your face was as calmly beautiful as if it were of marble. May I beg you—rest it again on the step in that way."